"Having interviewed hundreds of professi[onals] from the military or government sector, while they are all highly capable, they have limited operational knowledge in many areas, much like private security professionals would if they were entering government service. Carlos hits many points that will ease the transition from public to private and help demystify the corporate security world. If you truly want to 'get into security,' then this is a great starting point!"

— John Lineweaver, Regional Data Center Security Manager

"Can the transition be a scary process? Not if you plan your exit strategy and prepare yourself! The first step is purchasing Carlos Francisco's book *So, You Want to Get into Corporate Security?* It provides an all-encompassing guide to the transition into corporate security and instills confidence, preparation, and ultimately success! Coupling this book with Carlos' podcast *The Corporate Security Translator* will assist all levels of law enforcement, from the rookie to the seasoned officer close to retirement."

— Ryan Erwin, General Manager of Marksman Security Corporation and Former Assistant Chief of Police

"I've worked with thousands of people during their career transitions, including many military veterans and law enforcement officers. When they ask how to get ahead in their corporate job search, my most important advice is always to talk to an expert in the field, and Carlos is certainly an expert. *So, You Want to Get into Corporate Security?* is an insider's point of view with a wealth of resources for professionals at any job level who want to work in the world of corporate security."

— Scott Vedder, Fortune 100 Recruiter and Bestselling Author of *Signs of a Great Résumé* and *Signs of a Great Interview*

"Although I have some background in Executive Protection and Law Enforcement, as well as being a career Firefighter, so much has changed in the corporate world since I left it 23 years ago... Transitioning from an environment of rigid rules and regulations (like in the military, a fire department, or police department) into today's corporate world is daunting to say the least. As I enter the last five years of my government career and am considering my options, I now have a clear picture of what it will look like if I choose to go down the corporate security path. This book will help guide my decision in many ways."

— Drew Whyte, Firefighter/Paramedic, Arson Investigator, former Executive Protection agent (RST)

"In the year prior to my retirement as Division Chief from a large Sheriff's Office, I began the process of preparing for the next step in my career, which initially was to be a police chief. First step was to research the do's and dont's of becoming one. There were several resources available from the Chiefs of Police Association and the Police Executive Research Forum (PERF) but nothing was readily available for diving into the private sector. *So, You Want to Get into Corporate Security?* offers practical nuggets of advice for anyone coming from government to the private sector... Carlos has provided an excellent guide for maneuvering the nuances of the private sector's security operations. I highly recommend it for those looking toward the next phase of their career."

— Rickey Ricks, retired Division Chief with the Orange County Sheriff's Office and retired Security Area Manager with Walt Disney World Parks & Resorts

HOW 2 CONQUER

So, You Want to Get into Corporate Security?

by Carlos Francisco

HOW ②CONQUER

Published by How2Conquer
1990 Hosea L. Williams Drive NE
Atlanta, Georgia 30317
www.how2conquer.com

First edition, June 2021

Illustrations by Telia Garner
Book design by Emily Owens
Edited by Katherine Guntner

Printed in the United States of America

Library of Congress Control Number: 2021934511

Print ISBN: 978-1-945783-13-5
Ebook ISBN: 978-1-945783-14-2

This book is dedicated to:

My beautiful wife Joanna and new baby Jax. My dear mom, who fought through many difficulties and adversity to get me to where I am today. My big brother Frank and little sister Gabi; my childhood and military friends Roger, Danny, and Scott; and all the great leaders and educators who have shown me the way through tough times and in moments when I needed a lending hand. Thank you!

Contents

Contents

Introduction

First, I'd like to thank you for purchasing this book. This book is a combination of many years of hard work and sacrifice in an industry that continues to evolve and grow. Corporate security is a niche profession, and that makes things complicated for people who want to join the ranks. Being a security professional takes nuanced understanding of why corporations make the decisions they do in their protection — everything from staffing to post orders to the incredible complexity of video surveillance, intrusion detection, access control, and so many of the aspects of physical security in a corporate environment.

Over the past few years, as I've moved up the ladder of responsibility protecting some of the biggest global companies, I've had conversations with friends — remarkable leaders in their own right — that have shown me just how hard it is to grasp the intricacies of corporate physical security. It used to be that someone coming from the military, law enforcement, or any of the federal service areas had a leg up in their transition, but what I hear from my colleagues today is that the learning curve has become harder to navigate without a leader to set the course and help guide entry into the field.

My purpose for this book is to diminish that little feeling you have in your gut that tells you it will be too hard to translate what you knew and experienced in the military, law enforcement, or federal service into a career in the corporate world. I hope this book gives you an idea of what you need to not just fake it until you make it, but to step into a corporation feeling confident in your abilities and prepared to take on any tasks presented to you. I'll break down everything from fence line protection, corporate security standards and policies, overall security guidelines, post orders, and even emergency management. You'll learn the exact lessons that helped me transform from a young security officer working a back-entrance gate on the graveyard shift to a director level at one of the biggest companies in the world. I hope my 23 years of experience with major corporations like the Walt Disney Company, Amazon, and Facebook; and major events such as Super Bowl 50, Major League Baseball events, National Basketball Association games, and World-Class Marathons will give you a little bit of an edge to enter the corporate world with confidence and thrive in a new role in physical security. This information will prepare you for the interview processes, your first day on the job, and take you "to infinity and beyond!" (Oops, Disney's creeping back in!) By the end of this book, you should speak the language of physical security almost as if you've been in the corporate world your entire career.

I give you this information from the bottom of my heart and with respect to all the men and women who protect me, my family, and my loved ones globally and here at home. I wrote this book as a small repayment to all the great military, law enforcement, and federal folks I've had the opportunity to have as my leaders and who, with open hands and hearts, gave me all their knowledge in return. I hope you receive as much joy from it as I did while writing and that when you're done with this book, you feel prepared to tackle the physical security world in any corporation.

Now, turn that page, and let's start getting you ready for your next career!

Advice from my friend, Rickey Ricks,
retired Division Chief with the Orange County Sheriff's Office and retired Area Manager with the Walt Disney Company:

"The fact that you have spent a lifetime helping others by providing security to your community always came with the knowledge that the law stood behind you. Your value originated with the authority of the government, allowing you to intervene and remove criminals from society. That altruistic part of your career is now set aside for the benefit of a private entity. The ability to call upon the resources available to you for years may no longer be appropriate.

Moreover, a private company may not want some of those techniques utilized or resources tapped. Their long-standing methods may be just fine for them, and attempts to introduce new ideas may be met with resistance. Your new leaders may not desire you to have greater external influence than they do. It's possible that not everyone will be excited about your arrival."

Part I: Get Ready

Let's Get You to Your New Career!

I'm not sure what kind of work you have done so far to prepare for your future, but you might want to start thinking about doing a couple of essential things before initiating a career transition. Like almost everything in life, one of the most crucial steps is preparation. As you start thinking about your next career, it's a good idea to start planning three to five years before retiring from your current position. If you're one to three years away from making the jump, or even under a year, don't worry. This book will still work for you.

Remember, it's always best to look for a new job while you still have the old one. My mom told me that once when I was ready to quit a job but didn't have another lined up. Trust me, I stayed in that job until I found another one. I always listened to my mom — because she was always right.

The last thing you want to do is retire from your current career and spend months trying to get into your second. Many can afford a break, but many can't. Transitioning from the military, law enforcement, emergency services, and federal careers will be an exciting journey — you'll be thrilled and scared at the same time. But even if you're extremely eager to move on to your new career, there's no reason to make the adjustment any more nerve wracking than it already is.

Not much different from how I felt while writing this book and waiting for it to go out into the world!

I'm sure you've heard before that it's not where you go, it's how you get there. The same is true for switching up your career. Enjoy this journey as much as possible. Focus on thoughtfully executing one step at a time, and let the journey direct you to the outcome. The path will challenge some more than others. If it's easy for you, congrats! If it's tough for you, don't ever give up, and remember you are not going through this change alone. Phone a friend, reach out to new friends, and remember, I want you to get into corporate security. Reach out to me!

Chapter 1: Take Stock

Is corporate security for you, or should you think about something else?

In my conversations with colleagues, friends, and mentors, I've learned that there are three factors to consider before joining the corporate security world — or even before deciding if the job is right for you. Think about your personality, family, and goals. Going into corporate security is a big step in your continued career, and it has to be measured, evaluated, and weighed against your own values. Remember, physical security is *not* for everyone.

Consider a Personality Test

Before you kick off your corporate security journey, take a few personality tests. A personality test can help you figure out who *you* are and, from there, what kind of work is going to suit you. Maybe you entered the military or law enforcement as a young person who didn't really have much self-knowledge, but now you've lived a while, and it's time to figure yourself out.

There are plenty of free tests online (and some that you must pay for), such as:

- Myers-Briggs Assessment
- The free 16-Type Jung Personality Test
- DISC Assessment
- CliftonStrengths 34
- High5 Test

These types of tests won't just give you an idea of where you land in terms of personality, but they might also help you understand what drives you a little better.

Suppose your personality is one where your mission is everything. In that case, your squad is your family, and you would die for them. Or your work strength is gathered by operating weapons, kicking down doors, and being relentless about fighting a "bad guy."

If this is you, corporate security may be a challenge.

My incredible friend Altaf, a Marine Intelligence Officer and someone who has deployed in multiple theaters of war, told me that corporate security has been difficult for him because he can't find his mission. He goes to work every day, longing for the days when he was in constant lifesaving mode, preparing for an attack, living among his squad members, and knowing exactly what his mission was.

There are ways to find your mission in corporate security, but if you're like my friend Altaf, it might take a little more effort to see it. And we don't do guns or kicking down doors, so if high exhilaration action is what gets you up every morning, the corporate security world may not be for you.

Check out my YouTube channel, *The Corporate Security Translator*, for more about finding your mission in corporate security.

Do yourself a favor and get to know yourself better. Some companies give personality tests as part of the hiring process anyway. Wouldn't you rather know what the test is going to reveal before the hiring manager does?

Factor in Family

If you have a family, understanding what their goals are is vital. Have a conversation with your partner and kids about what the future looks like to them. As we get older, at least in my case, family becomes more important and your career starts to play second fiddle. There have been multiple times that I wanted to move out of California to greener pastures, but my family kept me here. See, I just caught myself as I wrote, "my family kept me here." It's not easy to say that, because it's hard to take so many people's needs into account when making a major decision about my career. The truth of the matter is that moving out of California today is not the right choice for my family. It may be the right one for me, but not for my family, which has become the most important part of my life.

My good buddy and mentor, Rhett, pointed out on my podcast how important it is to check the family's pulse first. He asked, "Who are you doing it for?" Think about that question. The last thing you want to do is decide for your entire family what their future will be.

Many folks coming from the military, law enforcement, emergency services, and federal careers have families that have given them 20, 25, 30-plus years of their lives for that first career. Take the time to ask them about what they want and share what you're thinking about doing after you retire. It will save you plenty of stress later in life.

Goals: Establish Your Why

To continue to expand on Rhett's question of who you're doing it for, we need to talk about goals. We all set goals at different times in our lives. Sometimes we can accomplish them, sometimes we fail, and sometimes we totally forget that we set a goal in the first place. Start asking yourself some of the following questions to help you develop your goal for the next phase of your life and career.

- Did you accomplish everything you wanted to achieve in life?
- Was your first career enough for you to retire and enjoy your family?
- Did you always have a goal to work for a major corporation?
- Is your goal financial, emotional, or simply because you need to stay busy?
- Did you ever want to start your own company? Be a police officer (if you are in the military or similar field)?
- Life goals are enormous things you have always dreamed of achieving. Will continuing to work at a corporation stop or delay you from doing that?

Maybe your reason is your family because you want to put your kids through college. It could be because one of your kids will be married soon, and you want to be able to pay for it. Or you could just want to purchase a home, etc.

Remember, you're not getting any younger. Could your time be better spent doing something else?

If your answers to the questions above land you right back at getting into corporate security, definitely keep reading. Even if it doesn't, keep reading. There might be "a thing or two about a thing or two" that you'll be able to use in other career paths, for the rest of your life, with your family, and even in your own business. And by the way, never stop setting goals, regardless of where you head from here!

Key Takeaways

In the lead up time to transitioning your career, spend some time taking stock of where you are, who you are, and what might need to change.

1 Personality tests can help you find strengths you might not know you have.

2 Knowing *why* you want to get into corporate security can be a powerful motivator for the journey ahead.

3 Make sure you're talking about your career transition with your family. They're part of the equation.

In the next chapter, you'll learn...

How to build connections with people in corporate security and in the corporate world. You'll need these relationships to help your transition and build a trusted network when it's time to make the move.

Chapter 2: Build Connections

My friend Tom told me all about his struggles to get into the corporate world after he retired from the Marines. Not being prepared was his biggest hurdle. He told me that his lack of corporate education led to no viable contacts, a horrible resume, and an inability to interview well; and it ultimately left him hanging without a job for over a year after he retired. He wished he'd had guidance or a roadmap to get him ready for what was about to come. He wished he'd kicked off his preparation years before he'd retired.

I told Tom that his struggles could benefit everyone thinking of retiring and transitioning from the military, law enforcement, emergency services, or federal jobs — because I was going to use them to create a plan to be used long before retirement. Using my conversation with Tom, I set out to put together a three-part plan to shift the odds in your favor. So, as you are thinking about retiring and transitioning to the corporate security world, start focusing on these three main goals:

1. Be everyone's best friend.
2. Get cozy with the corporate types.
3. Find buddies in security associations and trade groups.

Goal 1: Be Everyone's Best Friend

Aiming to be everyone's best friend is a sure way to expand your network. This philosophy will help you start your new career in corporate security with a strong web of contacts to get you a leg up wherever they can. I'd start by figuring out who around you has one to three years left in their current career and is about to retire. I bet they went through the same process you're about to start. Talk to them and pick their brains. Invite them out for lunch or a coffee. Ask if they'd be able to join you in a video conferencing happy hour for a drink and to talk about the future. Look for those folks and start asking them questions about what they had to do to prepare for their new career. Who did they talk to about their resume? What was the process of preparing for a corporate interview? Is there anyone else they think you should speak with? Are there any organizations that can help you through your transition? Do they have any contacts in the corporate industry that you can benefit from? Those are some of the questions I'd ask the people around you. Beyond that, I hope you've always been a friendly coworker so you can stay in contact with former workmates (and ride their coattails into your second career.)

Let's say you're not a nice person. (That can happen.) I highly suggest you change your ways and start to be an awesome coworker. Check in more often, say nice things to your teammates, take a genuine interest in them, ask to learn from them, ask for their feedback, and start positioning yourself as a desirable colleague to share an office with. The folks who are retiring today could easily be hiring you three to five years from now.

My good friend Roger has had great success with his "everyone's best friend" persona. He's currently a Lieutenant Colonel in the Army and consistently stays in touch with me, especially because he's retiring in the next five years. It almost seems like he's put me on his calendar since I usually hear from him about every month or so. He checks in to see how I'm doing, to ask questions about the security industry, and to ask about my family and little Jax, but most importantly, he goes deeper than the old "the weather is great" conversations. Roger has used our time together to always stay positive, make me feel good, and show that he would be an awesome partner to have around the office in the future. Though he has made a couple of jokes about riding my coattails when he retires (and trust me, I know he means it), I will gladly help him out when the time comes because he has put time into our relationship.

Take a page out of Roger's playbook and stay in touch with those soon-to-retire colleagues. Make sure you check in with them via social media, phone calls, or an email at least once every six months. When you check in, don't be afraid to get personal by asking them how their families are doing. If you can remember their kids' or spouse's names, don't be scared to use them in your conversation. People love to be called by their names, and they care even more when you remember the names of their family members. These are folks you'll go to when it's time for you to retire; they'll be your primary sources of assistance in your next career. These are folks who know how you work, remember how incredible you were as a team member, and will be willing to vouch for you when the time comes.

I've stayed in contact with multiple people from my Disney days and have been able to help in their next careers. The ones I truly pushed for were the ones who made the effort to stay in touch. They're the folks who have thanked me throughout our relationship, whether I gave them some helpful feedback or was just being a good listener; the ones who knew I was leaving Disney and asked a lot of questions when I was on my way to Silicon Valley and my second career; the ones who went deeper than surface chat about the weather in our conversations; the ones who stayed engaged with me, called to check on me and my family, and really cared about me and how I was doing. They're the ones I was most excited to have the opportunity to hire or help hook up with their second careers.

Goal 2: Get Cozy with the Corporate Types

When I say everyone's best friend, I mean everyone. Befriending corporate representatives has helped win many transitioning folks a career. It doesn't matter if you're in the military, law enforcement, federal jobs, or emergency services. Anyone from the frontline Security Manager all the way up to the CEO can easily be the one hiring you in the future, so you want them to remember you well! The goal here is to show them the utmost respect while you slowly become an ally they can count on. You need these folks to respect you and see what you're all about. Every time you meet with them, showcase the best version of yourself.

If you're in the military or a federal job, this is a great time to reach out to corporate leaders in your circle and ask if you can come by for a benchmarking trip — a trip where both of you exchange information about your operations to help both programs grow. This approach allows the leader of all the companies around you to observe your professionalism and how you work. Ask them how you can become a better partner. Take the time to listen to what they are saying, and when the opportunity arises, let them know a little bit about you. Be a good listener, and look for ways you can help them. Connect back with those leaders for lunch or breakfast so you can pick their brains. Very few people turn down free food, and it's a great opportunity to engage them and ask about the corporate world. You'll hardly find a corporate leader who wouldn't take the opportunity to learn more about you and what you do and, at the same time, give you feedback. People in the corporate security industry love to help, but I should warn you that many love to talk as well. Here I am, writing a book! Let them talk; leaders love to feel heard. Remember, the goal is to create a relationship that may be fruitful for both of you in the future.

If you're in law enforcement, fire rescue, or emergency services, make every call you respond to the best customer service call ever. Don't just make a "routine call" (especially if it's a major corporation you'd like to work for one day). Bring your "A" game when it comes to caring. When communicating with the company representative, always be respectful, no matter where they are on the corporate ladder. If the department you work for offers free classes to the community, offer to share more info with them. If you have time to stop by and introduce yourself while not on a call, do it. If you can occasionally drop in just to say happy holidays, even if it's just to the front desk person, do it! Your kindness and professionalism will shine through and could get you a job there in the future. I'd like to work with you!

One of my good friends is a Deputy Sheriff in Florida, and I had an opportunity to work with him while I led the day shift security team at Disney's Hollywood Studios. While working his beat, Vinny always stopped by the office to say hello and chat about life. He caught on right away that I loved collecting challenge coins. He was a big fan as well, so the conversations always seemed to start there. He was even nice enough to get me an Orange County Sheriff's Office coin that I treasure to this day. Every time we'd have to deal with an issue, Vinny was there to help. He always understood not only my needs, but the company's needs as well. He never ended a call without asking if there was anything else he could do for me. He always suggested free classes or training that the Sheriff's Office was offering and never failed to stop by my office to wish me happy holidays. Vinny was always there to help me and let me bounce ideas off him. It was never about him, his uniform, the title he held, or his badge and gun. It was about me, and that made me feel awesome. I would hire him in a heartbeat if he asked. Be like Vinny: Find a connection, and create an everlasting relationship that will get you the job in the future.

Remember, every call where you have to deal with a corporation is an opportunity. It'd be best if you used those interactions to showcase who you are and create new relationships. If you treat those calls like they're just another thing on your schedule, that corporation will treat you like just another applicant. So bring your best community policing!

If you're in the military or a federal job, these are perfect opportunities for creating private and government partnerships. Demonstrate your best customer service approach; don't squander your shot by acting like you're in charge. Trust me, all Security Managers and company leaders already know you're in charge. Make them feel that they're in charge and you want the best for their company and them.

Goal 3: Find Buddies in Security Associations and Trade Groups

One of the biggest mistakes transitioning folks make is not connecting with anyone outside of their field of work. And it's totally understandable. It's easy to just hang with your fellow squad members, battalion, fire house, etc., because you talk the same talk and walk the same walk. It feels safe; it keeps you away from headaches and judgment from outsiders. Well, I hope after you read this section, you'll think twice.

The corporate security field is as close as it gets to what you're doing today. That said, there are multiple security groups and associations you can join before you retire from your current career, and there are plenty of security-based certifications you can attain before you leave your field. I can't stress this enough: Being part of a security group or an association *before* you leave your current career is extremely important for your future. In any security, safety, investigation, or other related association, you'll be connected to thousands of people who have been doing corporate security work and, like you, transitioned into those roles. I bet you'll meet someone who knows someone you know. Our industry is the epitome of "it's a small world." (Yup, Disney pun intended!)

When I moved to California, I didn't know many people in the security industry on this side of the country. Since I was a member of ASIS, my first thought was to join a local chapter and head out to one of their meet-and-greets. At those events, I met many corporate security practitioners who are my dear friends today, as well as the "who's who" of the local security industry. I was guided toward companies that were the future of security technology and ready to go to market. I was invited to seminars and conferences, connected with local law enforcement and federal liaisons, and I even got to see some amazing speakers who are leading the way in our industry. See, it still works for me today as I continue to evolve and learn. And in the middle of meeting great new friends and companies, I scored some free drinks and dinners!

When you join, you'll learn, collaborate, and have all the educational resources you'll need to become prepared for the corporate security industry. You'll be able to follow the latest trends, innovations, and global developments. You'll be able to figure out if you'd like to work for a contract guard force or stay focused on corporations. ASIS, as with many other security groups, holds meetings, classes, certifications, and corporate-based security conventions throughout the world. Going to those events, becoming educated in the corporate security field, and making friends along the way can only be positive.

Security associations like ASIS offer ways to learn and focus on the elements of corporate security you may lack. You might learn about intrusion detection systems, cameras, access control, fence line security, Crime Prevention Through Environmental Design (CPTED), or any other of many security systems. Attending a meeting may guide you to different lines of business within corporate security, such as emergency management, business continuity, resiliency, corporate risk, investigations, asset protection, and executive protection, to name a few. You may even get a glimpse into the world of corporate security standards, policies, procedures, guard force contracts, security budgets, and so much more that dictates what corporate security is like today.

As you may have seen, I am a Certified Protection Professional (CPP). I received my certification through ASIS International. I highly recommend you look into getting some type of certification. When I received my CPP, I became much more marketable to hiring managers. These certificates indicate to corporations that you're educated for the opportunity they're offering.

Here's a few security associations you should check out:

- ASIS International
- Security Industry Association
- Electronic Security Association
- Security Industry Alarm Coalition
- Information Systems Security Association
- National Association of Security Companies
- International Security Management Association
- International Foundation for Protection Officers
- The National Council of Investigation and Security Services
- The International Association for Healthcare Security and Safety

The goals I've outlined so far are intended to set you up for success. You'll start to identify the industries that may be of interest to you. You may realize that you enjoy the people or the culture at a particular company and set your goal to work there.

Or you might realize that corporate security isn't for you. That's why you must begin to work through your transition process as soon as possible, so you can gather all the intelligence you need to be successful.

I have a buddy named Gerald, who used to work for the Alameda Sheriff's Office in California. Right around his eight-year mark with the Sheriff's Office, he told me he was getting tired of working in law enforcement. I gave him this three-part plan, and he followed it to a T for about two years. What he ended up realizing was that he didn't dislike working in law enforcement; he just disliked working at the Sheriff's

Office. Instead of moving toward corporate security, Gerald decided to apply for the FBI and, eventually, got in. We catch up now and again, and he always tells me that it was the best decision he made. Gerald was not ready to stop kicking down doors and running after bad guys, so the people he spoke to, the mentors he gathered, the meetings he attended, and the groups he interacted with helped guide him toward a different career transition.

Key Takeaways

Making connections with people already in corporate security should start well in advance of your career transition. You can also connect with people outside of security and leverage their expertise in helping you build a good network.

1 Reach out to your friends who have already transitioned to a corporate career. They're often happy to help another person with the transition.

2 Join security and trade associations in advance of your retirement or transition. These associations provide great networking opportunities via message boards and chapter events.

3 Get comfortable with being proactive and treating everyone like your best friend as you build your network.

In the next chapter, you'll learn...

How to set yourself up for success with some skills you'll need, like writing, public speaking, and learning new things.

Chapter 3: Time to Learn

Technology in today's world is everything! Later in the book, I'll break down security systems and data further, but this chapter is about the technology you should already know so you can have it on your resume.

The last thing you want to do is lie on your resume about knowing Google Docs, Microsoft Office, Dropbox, OneDrive, Splunk, or even Java, when you don't know any of them. Don't get me wrong — I'm not an expert in any of the programs I just mentioned, but I know enough to get through. I'm also aware that if I don't know, there are plenty of companies out there giving classes and certificates for these programs. And if I don't want to go that route, there's always YouTube!

Microsoft Word and Google Docs are staples in pretty much every company. If you can understand and work with one of those, it usually translates well to the others. You'll definitely need to learn how to use Outlook, Word, and Excel — all of those are critical to everyday business.

Analyze Your Writing Aptitude

Technical and personal aptitude are also part of this big corporate security puzzle. The days of having admin assistants who could do the writing for you are gone. Even high-level executives do their own admin work in most American companies. There's an excellent chance that you'll have to write a summary for your leader, Vice President of the company, or even the CEO. I know for a fact that if you're going for positions at Amazon (which are what they call "level five and up"), you'll have to showcase how well you write.

Brush up on your writing and don't just fall back on the report-writing skills you used in the military, law enforcement, or government positions; it doesn't translate well to the corporate world. You can also try out a writing assistance app like Grammarly. Yes, I pay for it, but it got me through my bachelor's and master's degrees, it helps me today in the corporate security office, and it has saved me from embarrassment more than once. It's worth it!

Get Ready to Speak

Honestly ask yourself and others around you about your speaking and presentation skills. There's plenty of that to be done in the corporate world, and you don't want to come off as a leader who can't speak or present. This isn't the style of briefing you would use to communicate with your chain of command in the field you're in today. Don't be rigid. Yes, get to the point, but leave a little room for some corporate flair! I love Ted Talks, by the way. After watching a few presentations, I got it! I was able to figure out an excellent format for presenting that would work for me. Check it out! You might find the same.

Be Willing to Learn

Admitting you don't know everything can be hard for some people. You really have to embrace being a student — even when it feels like you have enough experience to teach the class. Lots of your hard-won knowledge isn't going to be of use to you in corporate security (but lots of it will, of course!). Corporations (especially in tech and social) move really fast when it comes to introducing new systems and programs. The good thing is that for every new system or program, there's probably a YouTube tutorial out there that some nice person created. Get really comfortable with watching those videos, listening to podcasts, and finding other ways to soak up new skills.

You might be an old dog, but having an open mind about learning means there's always a new trick to master.

Key Takeaways

Take time to learn some new skills before you transition into your new career.

1 Familiarize yourself with programs that are staples of everyday business, like Microsoft Word, Outlook, Excel, and Google Docs.

Corporate communications mean you'll need to be fairly comfortable communicating through writing and presenting. **2**

3 Look for videos, podcasts, articles, and other ways to learn new systems and programs, and get cozy with the idea that you'll need to do it again in the future.

In the next chapter, you'll learn...

Your resume is what will get you into the interview room, so you'll need to take time to tailor it for your new career.

Part II: Resume, Interview, and Negotiations

Get into the Building

When I was growing up, people used to tell me that my resume would get me through the door. Later, I realized that it would get me through the door and right up to the interviewer. Today is not the same, and the corporate security industry has changed as well. There are thousands of people, all high-caliber superstars, going for the same position you are.

You have to differentiate yourself somehow, and not all of us have family members or buddies in high places to hire us. Yes, it's who you know, but I'll help you with that! If you have a relationship with someone inside the building, an "insider," your odds become much better. The process of putting in an application becomes a lot simpler. Now, to get to that insider inside the building, you'll have to navigate through the world of shaking hands and hugging babies. As I've said before, it's perfectly okay to reach out to folks on LinkedIn or similar sites to start a relationship.

Search for folks who work for the companies you'd like to join and follow them on LinkedIn. Send them a message, and see if they're willing to meet with you to talk about the company, the business, or your resume, or just for a meet-and-greet. When you meet with them, you want to bring your best abilities and attitude to the conversation. I'm not saying it's an interview, but trust me, they are evaluating you. After that initial conversation, keep in touch. Comment on their posts, and message them every couple of months to check in. Build a relationship with them, even if it's mainly online. Maybe set up another meeting to get reacquainted. Keep putting coins into that friendship bank.

After a few months, start checking to see if any opportunities are opening up within their company that could be a good fit for you. (The reason I say "after a few months" is because if you message them about an opportunity too soon after connecting with them, they will shut you off.) When an opportunity does open within their company, send them a message. Ask them for more details and what they think of it. Though you may think it's an opportunity for you, they might know something about the position you don't. Maybe that position is led by a horrible manager, or it does not pay enough, or it's based in a location you may not want, or it may even be filled already. No stress there. Keep the relationship going. When the next opportunity comes, ask again. Over time, you could build such a fantastic relationship that they may even reach out to you!

When you do find an opportunity that suits you, ask your contact if they'd be willing to give you a referral and/or submitting your resume for the position. That's getting into the building! Not only will you bypass the whole hour or so you would have spent applying, but you will be directly in the system and, most notably, the recruiter's hand. You're in! Hopefully, your insider was so incredible that not only did they drop off your resume in the internal system, but they also sent the recruiter or hiring manager a message about how awesome you are and why your resume should be on top.

That's how you pass the "resume algorithm police." It will be worth the time you put into it!

Chapter 4: Your Resume

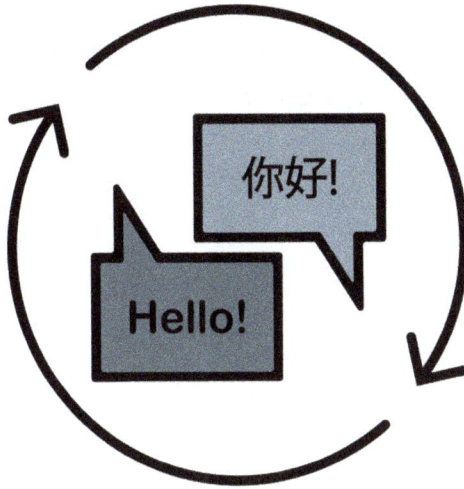

Hey! You're still with me! That's awesome. Now that we've tackled the "getting ready" part, let's concentrate on stepping across the first threshold — interviewing — and into the world of corporations and corporate physical security. As someone who interviews folks often, especially people like yourself who come from the military, law enforcement, emergency services, or federal jobs, these are the main things you'll need to focus on (along with the technical knowledge we'll discuss throughout the book). We'll go over your resume, researching a company, the interview process, and dealing with or negotiating the offer.

Career Change Resumes May Need Professional Help

I hope you've taken time to focus on your resume. I promise that your work experience will light up a recruiter's eyes and get them to look at your resume, but your resume is what will get you into the room for that interview.

Career change resumes are crucial to starting that second career in the corporate world. If you need help with yours, you can always look for books or online resources.

For further reading on resumes, I'd recommend *Signs of a Great Resume: Veterans Edition: How to Write a Resume that Speaks for Itself* by my good friend and former colleague, Scott Vedder.

If you can swing it, I'd highly suggest you reach out to a resume-writing company to assist you in writing an impressive corporate resume. The $50 to $200 that you spend will be worth every penny. If that's not an option, reach out to one of your friends who is currently in the corporate world. Buy them a coffee and ask if they'll review your resume.

Ditch the Jargon

You must be able to translate your prior resume into something human resources folks in the corporate world can easily understand. The jargon you're used to is specific to your current career niche, but it's not familiar to those in the corporate world.

For a guy like me who interviews terrific folks from the military, law enforcement, emergency services, and feds often, there's nothing worse than getting a resume that's full of jargon, abbreviations, and lingo I can't decipher. It's even worse when I ask the interviewee to explain to me what it all means and they can't explain it or translate it in a way that I, the corporate guy, can understand. Seriously, put in some time to convert your resume.

I once had a disastrous interview with an Army Colonel because I spent the entire time trying to decode his resume. As a result, I had no time to ask any questions other than the initial "Tell me about yourself" — which, by the way, he gave a terrible answer to. Line by line, the Army Colonel regurgitated the resume I had in front of me. I remember asking him about the size of the brigade he commanded, what his leadership structure was like, what an armored division was, what his budget was, what an O-6 was, what was covered in the joint professional military education (JPME) classes, and much more. It was exhausting. I wanted to tell the Colonel right then and there that I wanted to help him with his resume, but I couldn't for obvious HR/hiring reasons. I could understand that he had an immense background, but he did a terrible job translating it and getting me to understand his individual accomplishments. Everything he said was about the military. Needless to say, the Colonel didn't get the position.

Get Specific: Job Descriptions and Cover Letters

Take some time to look at the job description and try to mirror it in what you write. This means you may need multiple resumes that are *that* job specific. Don't take the approach that one resume will fit all corporate security jobs.

You'll need a cover letter as well. Even though most job posts today have online applications, many will still ask if you would like to attach a cover letter. I always read those. The cover letter often gives me a sense of who the person is before I even open their resume. It also shows me that the person took their time and took the application process seriously. It's even better when they have done some research on the hiring manager and addressed them on the letter.

Finally, just like with your resume, make sure the cover letter is tailored to the job you're applying for.

Perfection Matters

I'd hope that at this point in your career I don't need to mention this, but I will anyway: Format, spelling, and grammar are still important, so pay attention to those. Make time to read through and edit your resume and cover letter. In most cases, your resume should be no more than two pages, so you need to use that space carefully. Of course, if you have been in your current (or prior) career for a long time, a three-page resume may be understandable.

When you think it's perfect and as good as it gets, ask a friend to review your resume. They know you and, hopefully, know what your strengths are. A friend can sometimes see things you can't — especially when you've been staring at the document for a long time.

Time to Tell the World About You!

Once you get your resume in order and have shared it with a friend for thorough review and feedback, it's time to start looking at the company you want to work for and their open positions. But don't stop there.

LinkedIn is important these days. I have gotten two of my last three jobs from recruiters on LinkedIn reaching out to me, and I know countless others who have as well!

All the work you just did highlighting your achievements and translating jargon in your resume will help you create a really great LinkedIn profile. I'd also recommend using the website We Hire Heroes[1] as a resource.

Upload or copy and paste your resume into all the main job sites like Indeed, Glassdoor, Monster, etc. Each site has different requirements, and they change all the time. Before you upload, do a quick Google search for best practices for resumes on that site.

And don't forget — the corporate types and your new buddies in those security groups and associations are willing to boost your efforts. You can reach out to them with a very simple, non-spammy message like:

"Hey Carlos, great to connect with you (insert last time you talked or emailed). Just wanted to pass along my resume in case you come across a position that would be a good fit for

---

1 For help with your LinkedIn profile, visit: **wehireheroes.com/ blog/how-veterans-can-write-a-great-linkedin-profile/**

me. I've enjoyed serving my country, and I really look forward to using everything I've learned to transition my career.
Thank you,
Robert"

About Email and Signature Lines

As soon as you start your transition, you should have a professional email account and signature line. Avoid using an email address that is too personal or funny, or one with a username like "oorahbadass21" or something that includes your birth year like "deb1976." Create a free Gmail or other email account specifically for your job search so you can set your email signature, and your Uncle Henry won't get confused by an auto response asking him to check out your LinkedIn profile.

There are online signature services where you can build a really professional one with HTML (I like Email Signature Rescue), but you can also just set up something simpler within your email itself. No matter how you do it, here are some best practices:

Do's	Don'ts
Your name, first and last If you have professional credentials, like a CPP from ASIS, include the initials after your name. Don't include any degrees or other academic designations unless they're PhD level.	**Mailing address** No one needs to know where you live or how to find you.

Do's	Don'ts
Telephone number Recruiters and hiring managers might call you directly.	**Email address** It's redundant since the person you're sending the email to will have it.
LinkedIn profile A link to your profile is an easy way for them to check you out.	**Pictures/images/logos** It's not always a bad thing to include a picture of yourself (and a signature generator will even resize the image), but images can get flagged in corporate filters since they often contain viruses. Skip the image — they can see it on LinkedIn.
Profession, title, or tagline This can be a branding statement like "Security Professional."	
Personal website/blog Only include this if your website relates to your profession or job search. **Do not** include a website about your family, a hobby, or another unrelated topic.	

It's a good idea to test your email with a buddy. Send it from a variety of devices to a variety of devices. (Make sure you get someone who has an Android and someone who has an Apple product — they can each look different!)

Don't forget about the settings on your cell phone! Make sure outgoing emails sent from your mobile don't still have the "Sent from my iPhone 6" or "Please excuse the typos" note at the bottom.

About Voicemail

While you're taking the time to make a great resume and an email address with a sharp signature line, don't forget about your voicemail message. Make sure you record a message that is brief, clear, and professional with no background noise from children, pets, or traffic — and definitely no sirens, suspects, or superiors barking orders.

Example:

"Hello, you have reached Carlos Francisco. Please leave a message, and I'll get back to you as quickly as possible. Hope you're having a great day!"

Don't include "Please leave your name and number," because that will mark you as an older person. Modern mobile phones will tell you the number that called.

About Your Social Media

Hey, I know you're a real person with a private life, but when you're transitioning into corporate, know that recruiters and potential managers will check your social media. If you're coming from the military, you're used to having to keep your social media clean, but take some time to clean up your posts on public platforms like Twitter and Instagram too. Take control of the pictures you've been tagged in by friends and untag yourself in any that might seem unprofessional. That's sometimes a hidden source of images you might not want a recruiter to see. It's okay to showcase your life, but make sure what you're showcasing is deliberate and speaks to the best of who you are.

Key Takeaways

Your resume is a key artifact you'll need to spend time, and maybe even money, to develop. A resume is a door-opener and your first step to getting those critical interviews that get you into your new career.

1	Don't be afraid to get professional help with your resume. Very few people can build an attention-grabbing and professional resume on their own.
2	Avoid using jargon in your resume, especially if it's from the military or law enforcement.
3	Set up a professional voicemail and email address for your job search.
4	Review and clean up your social media. Set your profiles to private and exercise caution over your public comments.

In the next chapter, you'll learn...

How to target your ideal company, prepare for questions, and navigate the interview process.

Chapter 5: The Interview

So, you got the call, email, or text message and landed that interview. Congratulations! But you're not quite in the door yet. Remember, there are hundreds of people applying for this position. How deep do you know the company? What makes you better? What can you offer the company?

Know the Target

Before interviewing, take the time to understand the company culture. Read every post, follow them on every social media platform, learn about the leaders, and ultimately immerse yourself in the company for a couple of days. Use apps like LinkedIn to connect with some of the folks who work there. Reach out to friends who are already in the corporate world.

Usually, recruiters do an excellent job of preparing you with links to websites, culture, and even the interview process. Still, do your research! Find out about stock prices and the latest products or services they released or were part of.

Make Yourself a Cheat Sheet

Write it all down and make a cheat sheet. You'll be able to use this sheet throughout your interview.

INTERVIEW CHEAT SHEET

INTERVIEWER & COMPANY	CEO & MISSION STATEMENT	HIRING MANAGER

MATCH JOB DESCRIPTION	ABOUT THE COMPANY	YOUR TAG LINES

STAR METHOD

CARLOS FRANCISCO
THE CORPORATE SECURITY TRANSLATOR

Download this and other resources from the How2Conquer website! Check the **"Wrap Up and Resources" on page 137** for more info.

Go on an Interview Question Quest

Search YouTube and other websites for typical interview questions and guidance about how to answer them. I tend to take the top ten questions asked in an interview and use those to type out my answer to "Tell me about yourself." I read it multiple times before an interview to remind myself of where I want to go with my response and to keep it down to two or three minutes long, at most.

For your sake, please also have a good answer to other routine questions like "Why do you want to work here?" and "What makes you the most qualified person for this position?" There's a good chance you'll be asked one, if not all, of them.

Write your answers down and commit them to memory. The more time you put into preparing for your interview, the higher your odds of getting the position.

Here's a list of some of my favorite questions to ask:

- Tell me about yourself.
- Tell me about the partnerships you have been involved in. What did you do?
- What about key control systems have you used? What did you think of it/them?
- What intrusion detection systems (IDS) are you familiar with? What did you think of it/them?
- Tell me about the record management systems you have used. What did you think of it/them?
- What access control systems have you used? What did you think of it/them?
- What cameras and camera systems have you used? What did you think of it/them?
- Why do you want to work for this company?
- What is your leadership style?
- How would you secure my site?
- What's the most crucial piece of security?
- How would you deal with a problematic partner who will not budge on allowing you to implement a security feature/process?

- If I hire you, what will you do in the first 30/60/90 days?
- When it comes to security, what are you passionate about?
- How do you see yourself working with your internal and external partners?
- Will you be comfortable in the same position after five years?
- How would you go about implementing a security change to the operation?
- What are your weaknesses and strengths?
- Which do you like better: working on projects or managing people?
- What do you think is the most significant risk facing the security of our site and why? What would you do to eliminate or reduce that risk?
- If you had unlimited autonomy to make security operations at your site run more efficiently, what would you do and why?
- How do you keep your physical security skills current?
- Pretend I'm not a security person. Can you explain CPTED in simple terms?
- What strengths do you think are most important in a security leader?
- Can you tell me about a time when things didn't go the way you wanted at work, such as a project that failed or being passed over for a promotion?
- What are your favorite and least favorite parts of working security and why?
- What is your superpower? (Okay, I had to throw in a tech startup question!)

I also use a spreadsheet to help me keep my thoughts straight. It helps me answer questions while reminding myself of what I've done in the past. Here's one I've used before:

INTERVIEW TALKING POINTS

INTEGRATED SECURITY SYSTEM	Access Control	Cameras	Dispatch	Ownership	Social Media Monitoring
	Intrusion	Metal Detectors	CPTED	Safety	Written
				Programs	Keys to Sec. Systems
		Questions		Education	

CARLOS FRANCISCO
THE CORPORATE SECURITY TRANSLATOR

How Corporate Interviews Work

The kickoff to your interview musical chairs is about to start. I hope you put it all together, and you're ready to be the last one with your butt in a chair!

For each job you apply and interview for, you'll go through five to twelve interviews.

Yes, really.

In these interviews, you'll be asked everything from precise technical questions (which I will cover in later chapters) to weird tech startup world questions like, "What is your favorite color?" and "How does that color make you feel?" To the color question, I always answer blue and say, "Because it makes me feel happy." Just a suggestion. Never pick a dark color, and never give a negative feeling. In fact, never have a negative conversation or answer throughout your interview process. When it comes to your past employers, always stay positive.

The first round of interviews is usually with a recruiter or an HR person who will focus on what you know about the company. It will likely be a phone interview. Do your homework here. As I mentioned before, learn about the products and services they offer, what kind of company they are, and what market they play in. Look into how well their stocks are doing, what their mission and goals are, who the CEO is, who your boss will be, etc. Think about how you would be able to enhance their physical security and provide a benefit to their company.

If your first interview is via video instead of phone, do everything you would do for any other video conference. See the video tips later in this section.

The second round will probably be with the hiring manager or someone the hiring manager has asked to lead technical questions. Read through this book and get comfortable with the keywords. Familiarize yourself with the software, hardware, products, and systems I'll mention, and research further. Become super-educated.

This technical interview is the one that will clearly show if you know physical security and its systems. I'm not saying you need to become an expert on this journey, but you'll at least need to know the concepts and systems the interviewer is asking about.

I have plenty of stories where I asked technical questions and got answers that were nowhere close to planet Earth. Once, I asked an interviewee what he could tell me about key control systems. He responded that he controls keys in a box with a sign-out sheet. I then proceeded to lead him a little to see if he had worked with any other, more updated, tech-driven systems, and he stated, "It was not necessary." He didn't get the job. Another time, I asked an interviewee what he liked about analytical cameras after he told me how much he loved them, and he said that they work really well at night. Yup, that was it. He never mentioned anything about how they worked, what other systems they worked with, or why they were important. None of that! He left it at "Because they work great at night."

The third round of interviews is usually in person. With multiple people, they'll cover everything from culture fit to, once again, your knowledge about the business and how well you understand the job you applied for.

Ask the recruiter for some guidance on how to dress for the in-person interview. In some cases, the last round of interviews is with external partners. An external partner is someone who works closely with the corporate security department but is in a different area/department. Think of them as a client of the department, even though they work at the same company. Their job is usually just to figure out if you understand how important they are and to make sure you know that they are the client. In the corporate world, security is hardly the owner of anything. We are just a supporting act in this great play called Corporate Life. The goal at that third interview is to show the partners you'll be a willing and able participant in their business.

External partners want to make sure you won't impede their business, you understand their business, and ultimately, that you can create a security posture without slowing down their business.

Some Tips for Video Interviews

1	Wear professional clothing (but no suits — just look tidy, put together, and like you made an effort).
2	Test your camera and microphone ahead of time.
3	Check the invite for the platform they're using and make sure you've downloaded any required software.
4	Look at your background on camera. Is there anything behind you on the wall, desk, or bookcase that you wouldn't want to be seen?

Some Tips for Video Interviews

5	Try to be in a room with a closed door. If you have children or pets, you might want to lock the door.
6	Check your lighting at different times of day. An interview in the morning with full daylight coming through a window might make you nothing but a shadow.

About Dress for Interviews

I highly recommend you explore the culture of the company to decide how you should dress. Ask the recruiter what they'd suggest you wear. Mention that you would wear a suit and tie, but you're just not sure in today's world if they're a fit for this situation.

Tech companies, for example, tend toward more casual attire, so you wouldn't want to overdress. Leave those suits and ties for older companies, semi-government companies, or companies that work with government contracts.

Interview Mastery: The STAR Method

If there's an interview method that has rarely ever failed me, it's the STAR method. The STAR method helps you give the interviewer the full answer they want in a brief yet robust explanation, including how you deal with business challenges and how you succeed. **This method is excellent for behavioral or situational interviews, which most companies use today within the corporate security field**. You'll be competing with hundreds of people, and the interviewers will interview hundreds of people, so you need to stand out.

With the STAR method, all the answers you give must follow the Situation-Task-Action-Results pattern. Provide the context of a situation, describe the problems and challenges you faced, explain what you did and how you were able to solve them, and finally, give the results of the situation.

What are behavioral interview questions?

Interviewers ask behavioral interview questions to learn how you have behaved in previous work situations. In your answers, employers are looking for examples of your past actions that may predict how you'll act when you face these situations again. These questions are more open-ended than a "yes or no" question and usually ask you to share stories or examples from your previous jobs.

Many companies and hiring managers train their people to ask these types of questions to see if they can predict how you'll act if faced with challenging situations. The questions are usually more open-ended, and you can't answer with a simple yes or no. They want you to dig deep and share stories and experiences.

Behavioral questions can often trip up people who are more reserved or shy. They can be especially hard for those of us coming from the military or law enforcement because we're not used to sharing about ourselves and our challenges.

The STAR method can really help you avoid getting psyched out by an open-ended question that's designed to reveal more than you may be comfortable with.

So, what does the STAR method mean?

- Situation
- Task
- Action
- Result

Let's break down what each of these means.

Situation

In every question you're asked, you'll have to give the interviewer "what happened." What was the situation? Make sure you break it down and connect it to the work you have done. Or try to relate the situation to something you pulled from the job description, and connect it back to a situation you have lived.

Be specific to a situation rather than general with the responsibilities you had. It helps if you work on translating what you used to do to what you will do.

This piece is the intro to your answer, so keep it short — one to two sentences.

Example: "In my last position, I oversaw our vehicle fleet and had a minimal budget to work with, and many of our vehicles were reaching the lease deadlines. I had to find a way to make the budget go the distance."

Task

This is where you break down your involvement in the situation. Tell the interviewer what the mission was, what the goal was, and what your part in it was.

This piece should also be just a couple of sentences, at most. Place all your focus on no more than two points within your situation.

Example: "As the leader, I needed to make sure the team created a plan of attack. We took inventory; created a needs chart; worked on grading the vehicles from best, good, fair, to outdated; and focused on the outdated vehicles as our first approach."

Action

When it comes to action, break down your part in it — what you did and how you got over the hump. This is the step where you finally get a chance to go a little deeper, and it's also how the interviewer will measure you against all other applicants going through the same interview, being asked the same question. So, what were the significant movements you made to resolve the situation? You are the vital part here. You can start the sentence with "the team" or "we," but remember, this is about what *you* did. Keep it about you.

The situation you choose can have a negative outcome. The interviewer may ask you specifically to tell them about a project or a time when you led a team and dealt with a negative result. Use this process to break that situation down and make sure that you end the next step, the result, with all the positive lessons you learned from that negative situation.

Example: "I managed the project by having weekly meetings and setting goals such as timeliness, methodology, and approach. I guided the team in the processes, managed their time, allowed for creativity, and gave feedback when warranted. In the end, it was my job to present to the Town Manager, keep the project on time and within budget, and garner the best result."

Result

The result is just that — the result. What happened? How does the result tie back to you? Think of this as your closer!

Don't make this as long as the action part, but make it longer than the situation piece. Focus on your top results and what you learned. Remember, always keep it positive even if the result was negative.

Example: "The Town Manager loved it! By keeping the team focused and positive, and helping them through challenges, it was easy to present the outcome to the Town Manager while pushing daily operational information to the Chief. We were able to trade the outdated vehicles and pay minimum mileage overcharges, update the fair to last until next year's budget, and add a maintenance plan so vehicles would last longer. I learned the importance of communication and proper project management.

Take the time to examine two to three positive and one to two negative situations from your past in the STAR method. Write them out and commit them to memory. Jot down keywords that will remind you of the situation and the STAR method on your interview cheat sheet. There's a good chance you'll interview with multiple people, so you want to have multiple situations to use as examples if asked multiple times.

Putting It All Together

Example 1:

Question: Share an example of a time when you faced a difficult problem at work. How did you solve this problem?

Situation: I was the new security leader for the Great America Complex. When I arrived, I realized all the security officers were carrying handcuffs and batons. Coming from the Disney company and trying to create a softer approach to security, I had to find a way to remove those items from the officers.

Task: I knew I needed to make this right not only for the company, but for officers as well by removing those liabilities.

Action: I worked on a plan to gain the trust of the security officers and educate them on security methods and approaches for dealing with a difficult guest, and I also spent time educating the officers about liabilities. Slowly, I was able to change their hearts and minds.

Result: The results were amazing! We lowered the number of officer incidents, received more positive feedback from guests than we had ever received in the past, and through surveys, we found out guests also felt safer than in past years.

Example 2:

Question: *Describe a time when you were under a lot of pressure at work. How did you react?*

Situation: We had a special event at the park and needed to remove approximately 32,000 guests and allow 25,000 new guests to come in.

Task: The task was to lead this project with my small security team and make it happen flawlessly with no guest complaints or issues.

Action: I partnered with all the leaders from our various business lines to create signage for the entrance and different parts of the park to forewarn guests about the tight closing. We also made small fliers to hand to guests as they entered the park. I asked the leaders to assist and gave each of them positions in the park to help day guests exit, and I created a separate entrance for the incoming guests.

Result: The guests were happy with our communication and exited quickly at the end of the day. The private company that was renting out the park loved that we made their entire team feel special by creating their own entrance. By the way, the strategy was used from then on for both special events and everyday operations.

Example 3:

Question: *Tell me about a mistake you've made. How did you handle it?*

Situation: I was in charge of leading the security team during the mass exodus of vehicles from the Walt Disney property after the New Year's Eve celebration. I created roadway maps, traffic patterns, and cone layouts. However, when the night came, I realized I forgot to place cones at one of the major intersections.

Task: I took this very seriously and knew I needed to find a solution quickly because the backup was building, and vehicles were unable to move.

Action: After considering a few different ways to resolve the issue, I admitted my mistake to my boss. I informed him of my plan to add the cones to create a right-turn-only lane, easing the traffic and creating a continuous flow. I got in a vehicle, picked up several cones, brought a couple of officers with me, drove safely through the median with my emergency lights on, and placed the cones on the roadway.

Result: The plan worked better than I thought, and, ultimately, we were able to clear all the roadways faster than any other year due to the right-turn-only idea I had to implement on the fly. My boss was very grateful. I learned some incredible lessons that night about leadership, courage, and always leading with a can-do attitude.

Make sure your answers are honest and end on a positive note — even when they ask you for a situation with a negative outcome. Consider writing your stories down and practice saying them out loud, editing to make them shorter and clearer where necessary. While questions may vary, having at least three to five experiences to draw from will ensure you're able to deliver a confident response no matter what the interviewer asks.

STAR Interview Question Examples

Because I've done so many interviews — on both sides of the table — some of these questions might overlap with the list of my favorite interview questions included earlier.

- Share an example of a time when you faced a difficult problem at work. How did you solve this problem?
- Have you ever had to make an unpopular decision? How did you handle it?
- Describe a time when you were under a lot of pressure at work. How did you react?
- Tell me about a mistake you've made. How did you handle it?

- Share an example of a time you had to make a difficult decision. What did you do?
- Explain a situation where you used data or logic to make a recommendation.
- Tell me about a time when you disagreed with your boss. How did you resolve it?
- Describe a time when you had to deliver bad news. How did you do it?
- Tell me about a time you worked with other departments to complete a project.
- Share an example of a time when you failed. What did you learn from the experience?
- Tell me about a time when you set and achieved a specific goal.
- Tell me about a time when you had to persuade someone to do something.
- Describe a time when you had a conflict with a colleague. How did you handle it?
- Have you ever had to motivate others? How did you do it?
- Tell me about the last time your workday ended before you were able to get everything done.

Can I Ask Questions?

Yes! An interview is an exchange of information — you want to find out as much as you can about the company, just like they want to find out about you. What you don't want to do is ask questions that you should have found in your research (refer back to **"Know the Target" on page 38**). Here are some examples of questions you can ask your interviewer:

- What kinds of challenges should I expect to face in the first 90 days? How will success be measured?
    - This is a great question for a high-level position like a Security Director or Regional

Security Manager since you'll be held accountable for strategic directives that you help establish.

- Is there anything about my experience or background that might make you hesitate to move me forward in the process?
    - This is a good question to show that you're aware of yourself and your good and bad points as a candidate. Depending on the answer, you can try to counter the interviewer's perceptions, but don't argue!
- How does my background and experience compare to other candidates you're interviewing?
    - You might not get an honest answer to this question, but if the interviewer does mention an area where you appear weaker, you can give specific examples that show you do have the qualifications they are looking for.

The Last Word About Interviewing

Please do your best to make your answers and the experience positive. If your answer is not positive, be sure to focus on what you learned from the negative situation you're using as an example. With that advice in mind, I'm sure you'll ace all those interviews. I know the process of researching multiple companies and then interviewing numerous times can be challenging. However, the saying is true: "The more you interview, the better you get at it."

Key Takeaways

A successful interview strategy includes knowing your target audience, being ready for the questions you'll be asked (both general and security-specific), and knowing how to dress for and participate in video interviews.

1 Get sharp and ready with your interview clothing.

Really dig in and research the types of questions you might be asked, especially if you're targeting the tech sector. **2**

3 Master the STAR method.

Be ready to navigate the sometimes-complex corporate interview gauntlet. **4**

5 Be confident and ready to ask your own questions as part of the interview.

In the next chapter, you'll learn...

How to handle getting offers (and not getting offers) and the kind of negotiations that are expected in corporations.

Chapter 6: Negotiations

Getting the Offer

Look at you! You landed the position! You'll probably get a call to let you know that you landed the job, followed by an email with your offer. That's precisely what it is — an offer. That means you can counteroffer, which is something many people who come from the military, law enforcement, emergency services, or federal jobs are not used to, because there's just not an opportunity to negotiate in those fields. In the corporate world, the budget is not set by a government committee, and because a private corporation doesn't have to show how much they pay their employees, you should always think about yourself and ask for more money. Don't be shy. It's common to haggle a little bit; in fact, it's a given.

For the most part, each position already comes with a set amount of pay, but you can ask for a percentage higher than your current salary; try asking for at least 5% more than you're already making. Many companies today give out shares, especially in the tech industry, so you can ask for more stocks. Or you can ask for more money upfront, like a sign-on bonus or a moving bonus of some kind, or more vacation time.

You can even push back after the company counters, but maybe not too much. Whatever it is that you do, make sure you always counteroffer the first time.

One thing I will tell you is that if you got the offer, the job is yours. Don't be afraid to counteroffer thinking that you won't get the job if you do so.

It's vital to counteroffer because the price you start with will be the price that everything is measured against when it comes to bonuses, stocks, and opportunities for you to move up in the company later.

Not Getting the Offer

Look, we're not all perfect, and the truth is that you'll have to put in a lot of work to prepare for corporate security. You'll have to invest time in your background research, your resume, building your interview skills, and acing the technical aspects of the corporate security world. You'll have to spend time applying for multiple companies and possibly getting denied multiple times. When I wanted to leave a certain company, I applied for over 100 positions, created multiple resumes, was denied within 24 hours multiple times, and became discouraged. However, the love that I have for my family would not let me stop applying and interviewing. I just knew something great was right around the corner. I put a lot of my faith in a higher power and always believed that if I was given a real chance, I would knock it out of the park. You need to do the same.

Every time I failed at an interview, I became better. Every time I received the "thanks, but no thanks" email within 24 hours, I told myself that the position was not meant for me.

I also started to look at what I was applying for. I realized that I was so desperate to leave a job that made me unhappy that I was applying for anything, anywhere. I was applying for positions that were way below my capabilities. So I changed my tactics. I became more focused. I only targeted the industries I wanted, in the locations I wanted, in the positions I felt I deserved.

My mom always said, "If you know what you are worth, go get what you are worth!"

Little tidbits like that started to resurface from the back of my brain to keep me going. I became a better student and started to watch videos on YouTube that would help me master the interviews. I stayed positive and looked for ways to learn and grow. Do the same, and never give up.

You have to believe in the process and believe in yourself.

Key Takeaways

Getting an offer is exciting, but it's not the end of the journey. You can and should negotiate to get the best possible position.

1	It's expected that you will counter.
2	But counter carefully. There are some things that are negotiable and some that are not.
3	Emotionally prepare yourself to not get an offer. It can sting, but it's not the end of your search for that new career. It just means the fit wasn't right. There's a perfect fit out there for you.

In the next chapter, you'll learn...

In your first 90 days, you'll need to get a quick understanding of the corporate culture, how rank and relationships work, and how to be a leader.

Part III: Your First 90 Days

Take Your Time

It'll probably take the first three to six, or even nine, months to realize what you got yourself into. Even today, it takes me a good six to eight months just to understand a new business culture. The job I am in today didn't truly click until around the eighth month. Many of my friends have told me it's taken them a year or more just to feel comfortable in a new role. There's no need to hurry. It's a huge transition, like you've just moved to another country and you don't know the language or norms.

But even if the full journey to understanding *is* about eight months, you still need to really focus on your first 90 days — because that's what will set you up for success.

Chapter 7: What's Different About Corporate Culture

You'll need to prepare for the culture shift you're about to experience on the long road to corporate security. After you've worked hard to create meaningful relationships, now you must work hard to shift your mind to corporate culture. In the corporate world, culture is one of the most important nuances you'll need to understand. How a corporation moves, talks, and conducts business is attached to culture.

- You're probably coming from a **well-structured line of business** within some type of government entity.
- You're coming from a place where **you probably had step-by-step guidance** and procedures and policies on how to do almost everything. The structure was vital to your success.
- You're probably coming from a place where **they spent an outstanding amount of money on training you properly** so you can do the job right.

Well, the corporate world is just not like that. Everything moves fast, and there's very little time for anyone to spend educating you about the intricacies and culture of the business.

Seek First to Understand

When you go into meetings, be a listener. Think of it as the training audio you'd listen to during a commute. Observe the people in the room and how they interact with each other, almost like doing a human study. Some things you'll be studying may be quantitative but others may be qualitative.

- Pay attention to how meetings are started. Who leads the meetings? Where you came from, the highest-ranking officer may have been the one who always got the meeting started, but in the corporate world, many times it's simply whomever was asked to put the meeting together.
- Pay attention to who does most of the talking. Who does less talking? Who tries to always assert themselves?
- When do people smile? When do people laugh together?
- What is the corporate language?
- What corporate jargon and acronyms are being used? Use them yourself.
- How are presentations shown?
- How do meetings end, and who ends them?

All these nuances are important as you are learning in those critical early months.

Corporate Structure

The corporate world is open, and everyone is welcome to put in their two cents. This means decisions may be delayed or hard to come by because there are many folks in the room. On the other hand, in some corporations, you may be part of a very small team or even the only security professional they have. If that is the case, decision making can move quickly and directly to the CEO.

In some cases, physical security may still be part of the facilities department. Being under facilities poses a challenge on its own because all the decisions you make will be judged by an external party (who may not understand the physical security business) before they even get to the CEO. My friend Larry, a retired Army Colonel, told me a story about a time when he was trying to push forward what he called a "solid" camera plan, moving from analog cameras to digital. His facilities leader at the time was an old school kind of guy who thought that as long as nothing ever happened, there was never going to be a need for new cameras. It didn't matter how much Larry tried to explain the pros and cons, the value proposition, and the need to move to digital, his leader wouldn't budge. What Larry didn't realize was that it had nothing to do with money, efficiency, or better quality. He found out that the facilities leader was the one who had ordered those cameras a couple of years before Larry joined the company, and he was just trying to save face. But the facilities leader was also not up to date, so he was intimidated by the new cameras — even if they were more efficient and higher quality. This happens often when your leader doesn't come from a physical security background, backed by sophisticated security systems. Larry slowly gained his leader's trust, so when he suggested a couple of small tweaks to get the camera system changed over, his leader finally agreed.

Another block a security leader may find is that facilities folks need to be nimble and able to move quickly throughout a site. In many cases, these folks take care of the entire infrastructure of a building, so they need to get to an issue as fast as possible without impediment. But a security mindset is usually focused on creating fewer points of entry, more access control, and more accountability for everyone at a site. Well, facilities just doesn't see it the way we see it most of the time. You have to realize that there's a chance a leader you report to may not have anywhere near the level of experience you have in the field. You might want to take that into account as you look for your next career.

Why security and facilities are sometimes opposed: Facilities folks need to be nimble and move without impediment. Security has a continual struggle with openness. Security is about limiting or slowing movement.

Budgets

The struggle many leaders have coming from the military, law enforcement, emergency services, or federal jobs is that they rarely had to fight for a budget. Most of the time, it was just given to them. If this is you, don't sweat it. You can beat any corporate structure through education and data: Teach everyone around you, and have the proper data to make your case.

You'll need to get quotes from security vendors and security systems vendors, work with your procurement team, and set a plan. The plan may be a one-, three-, or five-year budget plan. Some of the items you invest in may go under the capital budget and some under the operating budget. You'll have to figure out your fixed costs compared to your variable expenses and even one-time expenses, like using a consultant. See? Not so different from what you already do at home but on a much bigger scale. I'll break this down more in later chapters.

Flat Organizations

Coming from the military, law enforcement, or a federal job, you are probably more familiar with a hierarchical organizational structure. Simply put, a hierarchical structure is like a pyramid, with each level reporting to the level above it until you get to the CEO/General at the top. The staff/lowest rank sits at the bottom of the pyramid, and they have little discretion over their job or assignments.

The problem with a hierarchy is that it can create rivalries between departments over resources, and there are fewer opportunities for communication and collaboration. Hierarchy creates a rigid structure that can develop over time to be averse to change.

And that's where a flat structure comes in.

A flat structure has few or no levels. Management and staff are mixed together, and people collaborate more. Departments, in theory, don't fight for resources just for themselves; they fight for them for projects that might involve multiple departments. The problem with a flat structure is that employees are sometimes confused over who they report to, and sometimes there are power struggles. A flat structure also has lots of people who are generalists (good at lots of things) and not as many people who are specialists (good at one thing).

Being a flat organization is a good thing for most major companies in today's world because it allows them to move fast and not lag due to a fast-moving market. That's almost a contradiction though, since in some corporations, everything must go through a barrage of people for a decision to be made. Moving fast is also the reason why many young companies make multiple HR and legal mistakes at an early age. They'll forgo removing a challenging employee because they're good at what they do, which always comes back to bite the company on the you-know-what. But employees are not the only issue you may come across with a flat organization.

At an early age, corporations just go! There's minimal vetting. When a major incident occurs like an active shooter incident, companies tend to jump on the ultra-security bandwagon without thinking about liability. After the YouTube headquarters shooting in 2018, many companies went out and hired every Tom, Dick, and Harry that had any type of weapons license to work at their campuses. They never thought about the liability behind it. Why not just hire local law enforcement to do the same job? Why have untrained, undercover folks running around your site with guns? One of the major roles of a corporate security leader is to always move liability away from the company. If you're going to be one of those leaders, always remember that.

Remember: Remove, deflect, and always pass the liability to any entity outside your company.

I digress! The point is that you may join a flat organization that needs everyone in the room to decide. Or you'll join one where you're the sole decision maker. The decision-making role will either be a tremendous task because you're with a new company learning the process, or it could be easy because they've been around for a long time and everyone knows their role. You may end up in a flat organization where autonomy is almost gone, and every decision you make will have to go through a body of internal and external partners. Or you are it, and all the decisions are yours to win or fail!

The Key is Being a Good Culture-Shifter

I'm lucky that I've been able to shift and fit into new cultures, and that skill has helped me tremendously in my security career. But don't fret! Even if you haven't had my experiences, you can learn how to culture shift.

Culture shifting is the act of changing how you appear to others in order to become part of a culture that is not natively your own. For example, wearing clothing that fits in with a group, using the language of a new group, adopting habits and ways of thinking that allow you to blend in. Culture shifting is not simply mimicking a culture — it's learning about the culture and figuring out how to be part of it.

I was born in Brazil, and I moved to the United States when I was 11 years old and planted my newly American feet in the little town of Guttenberg, New Jersey. I just happened to live on the poor side of town on the border of 68th Street and the town of West New York. My family had little money, so we lived seven deep most of the time in a two-bedroom apartment. No pity here, please. Those were some excellent times in my life. Being poor taught me to be creative and think outside the box. Well, I kind of had to. At the tender age of 11, I knew I had to do my best not only to fit into a new culture, but also to thrive. Kids were harsh at that age, so the faster I could blend in, the better. I didn't want to be the outsider — that guy who didn't speak English and, once he'd learned, had an accent — for too long. I knew then that assimilation was my key to success. Not only did I have to walk the American walk, but I also had to talk the American talk.

My dear single mom worked multiple jobs to keep the four of us fed with a roof over our heads. I remember her working at the Hispanic deli filling a type of Latin donut at 4:00 a.m. Then she'd come home to wake us up for school, go clean houses by 8:00 a.m., come back to feed us dinner, and then go deliver pizzas at Dominos until they closed. Hey, do you know what's great about closing a pizza shop at the end of the day? You get to take the leftover pizzas home for your kids! Man, I was tired of defrosting pizzas from the freezer, and for a long time, I was tired of eating them. Now, it's my favorite food.

My mom worked hard, so from a very young age, I had to work and be resourceful. I was the only kid in school who used to hate vacations because it meant I'd have to go clean houses with my mom. Later, when I was in high school in Florida, I had to wake up at 4:00 a.m. to help my mom clean offices before I started class at 7:15. None of my friends in high school knew that. I probably would've been embarrassed to say something then.

My wife would tell you that I learned absolutely nothing about cleaning from those days. (Insert your LOL here!) Little does she know that my lack of cleaning skills comes from the trauma of cleaning people's toilets and everything else at a young age. In case you didn't know from your own experience (which I highly doubt), people are disgusting. I guess my wife will know why I hate cleaning now.

I don't take those days for granted, and I thank my mom often for the early education. Now that I look back, it feels like it was some kind of FBI or CIA covert training, preparing me to blend into an enemy country. Many who meet me today would have absolutely no clue that I moved to the United States when I was 11. I worked on my accent to enunciate the American way, and I dove deep into the policies and procedures of my new country. Today, you could say that my accent is mainly a Floridian one with a hint of New Jersey on occasion, especially when I've had a great Kentucky bourbon or an American lager or two.

Those early days of hard work and helping family really taught me how to work through cultural differences and difficult times. There's a lot to be said about all the things I learned in those days, but I learned quickly how to become a chameleon in every situation.

You'll Need to Embrace the Chameleon

From where you're coming from, transitioning into the corporate world isn't that much different from my experience as a young immigrant. You're moving from one culture (in my case, a country) to another without tons of time to learn about it. It's almost the same gamble my mom took to make our lives better and reach for the American dream. You'll need to work hard too. You'll have homework — and often. Instead of cleaning houses, you might be catching up on some of the nuances of joining the corporate world at 4:00 a.m. before you go into work at 8:00.

You'll want to learn the key players you'll be working with, so start by going to your company's internal website and putting names to faces. Take notes about every corporate acronym thrown your way during the workday, then go home, break them down, and study so you can quickly speak your new language. Found yourself in a meeting about a security system you know nothing about? Well, take as many notes as you can, and when you get home, research. There will be unfamiliar cultural pieces of how business is done — and you might have to spend some time on those. All these nuances from your new country will be as important in the beginning as learning the business itself.

Taking the time to understand each difference and subtle distinction from the transition will make you an awesome chameleon and, ultimately, a subject matter expert in the corporate security field.

Jargon and Acronyms

Leave all the military, law enforcement, emergency services, or federal jargon from your past life behind — it's time to learn a whole new one! Corporate security jargon is usually based on a location, program, or team. See? Not much different than where you came from. Try to understand the corporate jargon—and start using it—as soon as possible. You'll be able to blend in quicker, and it'll make you feel more like part of the team. At the beginning, it may be awkward to use this foreign language, but soon enough, it will become part of your vernacular.

In one of the episodes of my podcast, my good friend and team member Greg, who is a retired California Police Chief, told me that corporate jargon was one of the things that confused him in the beginning. He was trying to change his language from cop to corporate, and he told me he would sit in meetings in the beginning, smiling as people threw corporate terms and acronyms at him as if he knew what they were talking about. When asked if he understood in these meetings, he'd just nod and say yes with a huge smile on his face. To him, it was about staying positive, being in the moment, and jotting down every term and acronym that came at him for his homework. In those times, he said that he'd spend a good hour hunting down the meaning of all the jargon just so he could get to the work. According to Greg, the key was becoming friendly with many of the folks he worked with right away so he could get the translations he needed from them. Make friends, and make friends fast!

The Open Concept Office

There are a lot of great things to look forward to, especially if you get into a tech company. The pay, benefits, stocks, bonuses, and free stuff will be fantastic. You'll have a cool fitness center with personal trainers and dieticians; spas to get massages and your nails and hair done; alcohol and happy hours at work; and snacks and free food galore. You might even be able to wear shorts and boat shoes if you'd like. (That's my personal style every day!)

But there's also a downside. There won't be closed offices since it's all about open spaces and hoteling (hotelling is just taking open desks as you arrive for work instead of having an assigned desk). You'll have to worry about information security more often. If you're working on something secretive, you might want to get some computer screen guards so people don't know what you're working on. Anyway, that beautiful office you once had that allowed you to close the doors and concentrate — it's gone. Get ready to work in a noisy environment with people coming to your desk for a conversation every five minutes.

The positive side of this is that everyone sees you, and you get a chance to see everyone. When your team members walk by, you can say hi and check on their families. When the partner you've been meaning to talk to about that important project walks by, you can stop them for a quick chat. When the boss walks by, you can say hello and stay relevant in your boss's mind. Trust me, it's not brownnosing in the corporate world; it's creating a relationship with your boss. Plus, it's the courteous thing to do. If you have your own desk, you could throw a couple of items on top of it that might act as conversation pieces — maybe a picture of the family or a miniature helmet from your favorite football team. I have challenge coins and mini flags of all the countries I've visited. The flags are always a hit! I've created great relationships around the office just because someone asked me about those flags.

Dress and Clothing

Men's and women's suits are slowly becoming extinct, especially at new companies that have only been around for the last 15 years or so. While dress codes may be more relaxed, it does mean you have more choices to make about clothing. My typical outift is shorts, a Cuban shirt, and boat shoes. It takes a while to get comfortable out of uniform, so I always recommend making your own "uniform," so you don't worry so much about choosing the right clothes.

Here are some items that will look good and keep you comfortable:

- Golf shirts
- Jeans
- Khakis – You can even press them with that crisp, knife-edge pleat if you'd like.
- Tennis shoes or sneakers – Most open-concept offices have concrete floors, which is why most tech workers wear sneakers. Leather-soled shoes can be slippery and hard to spend all day in when you're on concrete.
- Collared dress shirts – You may need them for meetings with vendors and big bosses (but observe what other people wear first).
- Dresses – Ladies can wear whatever makes them feel great. There's lots of leeway for wearing dresses or pants. Keep in mind the expected activities of the day if you're going to wear a dress, though, because even in a big corporate environment, security people are often all over the facility every day.
- Heels – Ladies, wear heels if you love heels, but know that on a concrete floor in an open concept office, people will hear you coming and going.

Your journey into this new country — the corporate security industry — is about to start. Get ready for a bumpy beginning, but I promise you everything will fall into place. As my old friends at the Mouse House used to say, "Please stand clear of the doors, put on your seatbelts, and keep your hands inside the vehicle at all times. It's going to be a bumpy ride!"

Key Takeaways

Corporate culture and the structure of a company can be wildly different from what you might be used to in the military, law enforcement, or federal jobs. Everything from structure to budgets to what you can wear has the potential to be disorienting if you're not ready for it.

1 Organizations can be very flat, especially in start-ups or the tech sector. But very mature organizations can be just as driven by strict hierarchy as any branch of the service.

The key is being a good culture-shifter and being able to fit yourself into the culture, because the culture won't fit itself to you. **2**

3 Managing a budget is something every security professional has to grapple with. Security is a cost center (meaning it doesn't generate profit for the company), so budgets will be an ongoing part of your career.

Ditch jargon and acronyms. **4**

Key Takeaways

5 Embrace having a desk right out in the middle of everything because open concept offices are the norm in most companies.

Develop your own version of a uniform that you'll feel comfortable in but won't set you apart from your co-workers. **6**

In the next chapter, you'll learn...

Relationships are more important than rank. And building relationships will be a key part of your success in a corporation.

Chapter 8: Ranks, Relationships, and Sharing

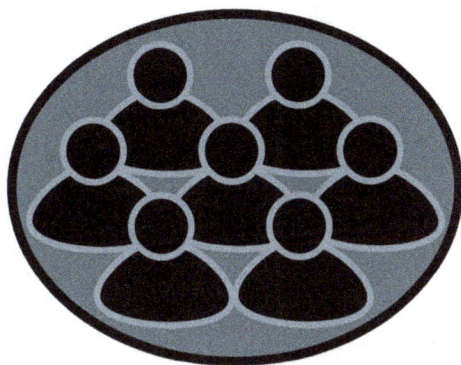

Rank Is Over

There's no rank in corporate culture the way there is in the military, government, or law enforcement. Everything is done through relationships. It's almost never okay to use "pulling rank" language like "Because I said so," or "It's an order!" Ranks, a lot of times, are irrelevant.

There's no more squad and shop talk, and no more calling someone by their last name or call signs that would indicate anything they'd done in the past. Welcome to first names! Show respect to the people who hold higher positions within the company, but by no means should rank ever come into play. If you're the leader in the room and you find yourself in a position where you feel like you need to show your rank, my suggestion is to play it cool. Never sit around and talk about what you were, how many years you have been, where you served, why you are the highest in the room, who in the corporation you are, etc. If you use those tools, the folks in the room will think *you* are a tool, and you don't want that. Always be gracious with anyone you speak to.

My team member Sheila, a director-level employee at the company I work for and a retired Secret Service protective intelligence leader, learned right away that rank is not a thing. In a one-on-one meeting we had, where we usually start with the niceties and talk about the past, she shared a couple of points on the rank topic. She mentioned that rank is so irrelevant in the corporate security world that when someone "pulls rank," that person is usually talked about for days, and most don't want to work with them after that. Sheila said that a leader in corporate security must understand that nothing can get done without the entire security team. It's your duty to prop up everyone around you and be thankful for the help they give. I told Sheila she was brilliant. Because she was right! Now you see how she became an intelligence leader in her past career.

Forget about your position in the company, and always use the word "team." Refer to your team and talk about them as if they deserve all the merit, as if you're just there to help them achieve great success. Your team always comes before you in the company. When adding your input in a conversation, you should go last. Let everyone else speak first, and take in what they say and learn. Lastly, if you're going to lead teams of leaders, who you are in a room should never be a point of contention with those you lead. Let them lead you and the program you'll be running. No ranks necessary.

Relationships Are In

Relationships are in and ranks are out. Like any good leader, you hope your team is following you because you're leading them, and not because they're scared of you or your corporate rank. Growing up, I had to learn a lot about leadership. At one time, I even thought throwing my rank around would get my team to do what I wanted them to.

I was young and naive then.

Now I understand the value of office relationships. I know what you may be thinking, but it's not that type of relationship.

The relationships I'm talking about are the ones that are nurtured through respect, appreciation, and valuing everyone around you for who they are. That kind of relationship takes a bit of work, but it's worth it. It has to be built with genuine honesty, empathy, humility, and the ability to be vulnerable. That's how you get things done at a corporation. Rank is an antiquated way to look at leadership — and definitely not the way to look at leadership in corporate security.

Fred Fuller and John Brown, some of my fellow writers at How2Conquer, wrote a really great book about relationships in business, and I highly recommend reading it. It's called *A Dragon Walks into a Meeting*. Guess what? We're all going to end up in a meeting with a dragon, and if you've done the work to understand relationships, that dragon will be pretty easy to tame.

CAUTION: Getting Friended by Your Coworkers

While you're creating meaningful relationships and becoming buddies with everybody you work with, should you add them on social media? I remember in my short time as a police officer, I actually shut off my Facebook and every other social media account I had. It was an unwritten policy that you shouldnt have one. In tech corporations today, being friends on Facebook is the norm. However, it's important to remember who your new friends are. Your page should be clear of anything that might shed a bad light on you, including nudity, religion, or politics, to name a few.

You don't want to put anything on your social media that you wouldn't want to place on top of your desk, in your office, or in your work locker.

Go over your social media feed and delete any posts that would not be acceptable in the workplace. You can even block content for work friends. Being part of social media with your work colleagues is more accepted today than ever, but be careful and always be conscious of what you put up. Before creating any posts on your feed, always ask yourself, "Can I show this at my office? Will my family approve of it? Will my CEO accept it?" There's an old saying my buddy Brent Kennedy taught me that I always think about in these situations: "You do as much as you think your career can handle!"

I had a close friend who happened to work for one of the big social media companies. He was retired Army Special Forces with many hours of combat duty, an impeccable sense of humor, and the ability to be liked by almost anyone. Like many these days, he became friends with a lot of colleagues at work and on social media. He worked for an open company, so he thought he could post anything on his feed. He'd seen many of his team members' feeds, and they added whatever they wanted without any repercussions. He felt he was safe. If they could put up liberal-driven posts, he felt he could put up conservative posts as well. Well, he got in trouble. The moral of the story is to pay attention to your surroundings. When a company says they're open and care about all points of view, do they really? Sometimes it's better to stay vanilla (as my niece says I am). Feel the temperature in the room, and for your career's sake, sometimes it's better to just go along with it.

Find an Honest Buddy/Mentor

Find someone who will tell you about the company culture and how to navigate it. There are plenty of these folks around, you just have to ask! You may have known everything in the past, and in those days you were the subject matter expert, but today you are not. Well, at least not yet! There's absolutely nothing wrong with that. I repeat: There's absolutely nothing wrong with that. Ask meaningful questions and be humble.

The best leaders I've ever had in my corporate security career were all folks who were previously in the military, law enforcement, emergency services, and federal jobs. They were humble enough to understand that they didn't know everything, and they were classy enough to let me know. Those leaders were the ones who moved up in their careers and, as you may know from your previous job, the leaders others would go to war for. They're the kind of leaders who can be honest enough to admit the reason they hired you is that you knew more than them. That's the kind of leader who will tell you to run the program while they move blocks out of your way. They'll be your fullbacks, blocking tacklers while you're running the ball behind them.

When I started as a leader at Disney, I had plenty of questions about what to do. Though I grew up in the company (and, from all accounts, was one of the best operators around), I had no clue what leadership at that type of company was like. I attached myself right away to two of the leaders who'd helped me become a manager. I thought since they helped me get in, they'd want to see me succeed, and they did. I constantly bothered them about the software we were using, the reasons why we led in a certain way, why policies were formulated and directed at a particular operation, how to act in front of cast members who had way more experience than I did, and much more. I'm sure they were tired of me back then, but today, they are my mentors and best friends. That's because I wasn't afraid to ask and let the world know that I didn't know everything. Guess what? I survived!

Don't Be the Know-It-All

You don't want to be known around the office as the person who dismisses other people's suggestions or opinions, the person who takes over every meeting, or the person who people just don't want to associate with. In the corporate world, everyone has a voice, and everyone gives their stamp of approval before moving forward with almost anything. Just remember, there's a very good chance that all those people in the room have a lot more experience in corporate security and probably know way more about it than you. The best thing to do is listen first and speak last. Pick out the smartest people in the room and learn from them. If you don't have anything productive to add to the conversation, just stay quiet and wait for someone to ask you a question.

Don't speak just because you like to hear your voice. Everyone in the room is probably comfortable that you don't know it all. If you're looking for acknowledgment or recognition for everything you do, ask your spouse to start a star chart on your refrigerator at home.

Like my buddy John Lineweaver always says, you must attach yourself to great, intelligent, and successful people if you want to make it.

There was a time I worked with a know-it-all. This person always wanted to assert himself as the expert in all things. He would speak out of turn, louder than anyone else, and frequently went on for what seemed to be hours. He cut people off, made everyone in the room feel small, and lost a lot of friends along the way. He couldn't get any of his projects accomplished, no one ever vouched for him when it was bonus or move-up-in-the-company time, and he always sat alone in the cafeteria. Don't be a know-it-all; be a listen-to-all! And when you do talk, pay attention to see if what you said was received well.

If your contributions are received well from the start, keep going. If they aren't, relax, breathe, and when you have a little time, ask your new honest buddy/mentor why your idea didn't work or why it wasn't received well.

The corporate world can be weird. You'll have to manage the give and take often in conversations or meetings. I guess you can always look for a compromise, though I've heard that even in that situation, someone loses a bit. Negotiating is sometimes part of the game, so try to settle in your favor. Go into the meeting already knowing what you want the outcome to be, and you can guide the conversation in that direction. In return, the people you're negotiating with will think they got what they wanted and that you weren't trying to ram it down their throats.

About Jokes and Stories

The jokes you could tell before won't fit your new corporate environment. Avoid all conversations about politics, money, religion, or groups of people who have been marginalized due to their skin color, religion, beliefs, gender, sexuality, etc., unless it's directly related to your role and essential for the corporation. An accurate and factual description of an incident is always okay. It's not okay to share your feelings about the use of "he," "she," or "them;" or bathroom use; or the President this, and the Democrats or Republicans that; or what you find in the men's restroom (like feminine products). Don't comment on things like this and keep your beliefs to yourself. There's a good chance what you say could be misconstrued, and it won't be translated well.

Positive relationships are everything, and you want to make sure you maintain those at all costs. Always be honest but kind. Feedback is a gift, but it must be timely and given with kindness and honesty.

If what you're about to discuss with an employee or boss feels wrong, run it by HR first!

By the way, human resources at a corporation is involved in everything. They're your friend. In the corporate world, their jobs range from recruiting and interviewing to being a parent to firing. Besides that, they deal with your money and benefits, and they make sure you have all the training you need to cover the company and yourself. They plan, direct, and coordinate all the administrative functions of your team and the company. They are the link between you, managers, and employees. If you ever have any questions or anything you're not sure about, just ask them before you make a fool of yourself and place the corporation in jeopardy. Don't be the person on the wrong side of a disciplinary procedure.

Internal Politics

I'm sure you had politics where you came from, but a lot of times, you could squash it or stay out of it because of your rank. Well, the corporate world is a little different. I'll use the **who, what, why, when, how** approach to break this one down. This might be familiar to all the investigators out there.

The **who of corporate politics is about who they are.** Who owns a project? Who is the decision-maker, and who calls the shots? That's one person you want to become close work buddies with. Usually, this shot-caller is working for the big boss, as you'd say on a Navy carrier. This project manager may even be called the "Captains' Sergeant."

What the project is about, what the company wants, or what the shot-caller wants — learn that, and learn it quickly. Projects are extremely important for a corporation, especially in the tech world, because they drive the company. They're what makes a company move fast. They're also how everyone gets measured — they showcase what you're worth for the company, and they're what gets you a higher bonus in the next cycle. Don't be afraid to ask the decision-maker what their end goal is — guessing sucks! Just ask how you can help them get to their goal as fast as possible.

Find out the why. Not just from the shot-caller, but also the company — their why is essential. Find out why the project should be critical for anyone below, around, and next to you. The why is super important for anyone who works in corporations.

You won't be able to say, "Because it's an order!" Trust me — it will never, ever work.

When is crucial because you need to know your timeline, but you'll also have to make sure your team and everyone around you are adhering to the schedule.

How it needs to be done. I left this one for last because, as mentioned before, you may be working for a company where everyone gives input, or in contrast, you may be the only person with input. Find out exactly how your company wants things done early. What resources do you have? Are there others who are involved in making decisions? If so, who? Are there limitations on what you can do or make decisions about without input from a stakeholder? The "how" is usually closely related to a company's culture, so ask questions and observe so you can master it (and avoid ruffling feathers).

Key Takeaways

Relationships are the engine that drives a company, and they tend to be more important than position or rank. You'll need to develop the strategies that will help you fit into this new world.

1 Carefully navigate getting friended on social media by your coworkers. It's bad form to reject requests; just make sure your social media is set up to be friendly for people who may not share your beliefs. You can still have those beliefs, of course. Just focus on your settings so some things are kept private.

2 Find a buddy or mentor — they don't have to be within security — who can help you navigate some of the stickier aspects of relationships in this new and unfamiliar world.

3 Exercise extreme caution with telling jokes or stories. If you wouldn't share the joke with your children or your mom, it's probably not suitable for the workplace.

4 Avoid internal politics to the extent possible and tread carefully when avoidance is impossible.

5 Take time and put emphasis on relationships by nurturing, respecting, appreciating, and valuing everyone around you for who they are.

In the next chapter, you'll learn...

Some companies have a very small corporate security footprint, and you may be hired directly into a leadership position. To prepare you, we'll explore a couple of solid plays that will put you in the power seat.

Chapter 9: What If You Are the Leader?

What if you are the new corporate security leader they hired? When you join a corporation as the sole physical security professional, what are you going to do? The thought may seem daunting as you read this, but I'll give you a couple of things to think about. So far in my career, I've seen:

- The buddy play
- The "I am the greatest" AKA the GOAT play
- The gaslight play
- The empire ME play
- The smart play

We'll break each of these plays down, but first — a story about buddies.

The year was 1533. King Securalos, of the great country and naval superpower The United Corporate Security, called for the best carpenters and boat makers to meet him. The King invited all of them to the capital Securityland, right on the beautiful north shore of the country. He asked them to make the biggest, strongest, and fastest ship they could, so one lucky captain and his crew could go out in search of a magical island the King had heard about as a child called The Answer. King Securalos had heard wonderful stories of what answers lay on that island. The carpenters and boat makers built him a great ship called Experience, and so King Securalos needed a captain.

The King needed a captain who could withstand years at sea and gain knowledge through Experience. The King chose Captain Hard Worker from the great coastal city of Humbleness, and the journey began to find The Answer. While out at sea, Captain Hard Worker came across the island of Risk Audit. A couple of years later, while on his journey, he stumbled upon the island of Security Standards. After a couple more years, he came across the island of CPTED, followed by the island of Security Systems. He was worried he would never reach The Answer and wrote to the King often on his travels about what he had learned. The King trusted Captain Hard Worker and encouraged him on. Captain Hard Worker found the islands of Security Policy and Procedures, then the sister islands of Guidelines and Post Orders, but no sight of The Answer. He continued traveling and learning. He came across a particularly interesting island called Security Training. What he learned from that island was incredible, and he knew he was close to The Answer.

Captain Hard Worker found the islands of Contract Guard Force, Security Operations, Corporate Investigations, and even Asset Protection, which used to be called Loss Prevention. He had been traveling for 20 years and had been to many islands throughout the world, but The Answer always eluded him. King Securalos was growing old and frail, but he still believed Captain Hard Worker would get to The Answer. One day, after many years on the vast sea, the Captain noticed a tiny island. The island was so small, it intrigued him. Could it be The Answer?

It was! Now he understood why the island was so hard to find. It was tiny, and the ocean was immense. He landed on The Answer, and right then and there, he understood the magic that King Securalos had described. "Knowledge!" Captain Hard Worker shouted.

The moral of the story is that to get to The Answer, you must go through all those islands first. Once you find The Answer, it's easy to navigate there again. If you haven't found The Answer, you may get there one day, but the ocean is vast, and the island is small. It may take you a long time. Think of your program as the journey Captain Hard Worker took. Iff you're a new leader in charge of the corporate security program for your company, make sure you bring a captain who has been to the island. Hire that aptain; they will make it a lot easier for you. They'll share all the knowledge they gained trying to find The Answer, and your program will be able to get to The Answer it needs a lot faster.

Buddy Play

You'll inevitably come across a lot of tough questions when you start your position. At the beginning, you may give amazing high-level answers, so high that many folks in the room will be intrigued — or wildly confused. So you'll reach out to anyone you know in the corporate security business and start asking them what you should do. Soon enough, you'll get a budget to hire people, and this is where the fun begins. You'll reach out to all the buddies you may owe a favor to and start hiring them for positions that are super intricate and technical. It's usually for positions in operations, security systems, a Security Operations Center (SOC), and even VIP/executive close protection. Usually, they have very little to no knowledge of the organization within your corporate security umbrella.

The issue is that you hired your buddy, who has less of an understanding of corporate security than you do, and you're asking them to lead a line of business. You'll have a lot of fun at work, but you and your buddies will c struggle and not be able to get anything accomplished without extreme pain and suffering.

Word of advice: Hire the best person you can get with the most years in the corporate world in that specific position. I promise you it will pay dividends.

As you grow, you can recruit your buddies for positions below the security line or business expert. You'll get to the island a lot quicker, and you'll still be able to repay your buddies for all those years they were nice to you.

"I Am the Greatest" AKA the GOAT Play

There's no worse leader (wait, should I even say "leader?") to work for than the one who thinks they are the greatest, they know it all, and there's nothing you can say or teach that they don't already know. The problem with leaders like that is they suffer tremendously from insecurity; they'd fail an entire corporation, a leader, or a team just to save face. They're incapable of being vulnerable, connecting, or leading incredible folks, so they hire inferior employees so they can continue to feel almighty and powerful.

The issue with the GOAT play is that you only hired people who seemed inferior to you, and you yourself just started in the corporate security world. Like the buddy play, you may feel good about yourself, but nothing will get accomplished. You and your team will continue to fail and not reach the goals set by your leader.

Word of advice: Stop being insecure, hire people that are better than you, embrace opportunities to learn, and make yourself available to some vulnerability. The world will be your oyster.

Hiring someone who knows less than you to run a program when you're still a novice will not only get you fired, but it'll surely doom the less-qualified person you hired. Don't be afraid to hire people who know more than you and let them run. They operate, and you politic! Maybe you'll learn a thing or two and get recognized as a great leader. Wouldn't that be nice!

Gaslight Play

The gaslight play is an interesting one. Many times, companies will have extra money in their budgets to bring in an expert. Usually, these consultants have many years of experience, have done consulting work for many companies, and their work comes with the insurance that they will get the job done well, within budget, and on time. So, you hire the consultant or consulting company and ask them to give you a plan of attack. To save face, the inept leader will do one of two things: They'll either take the consulting company's results and use them as their own, or they'll take the work done by the consulting company and throw it right in the garbage.

This kind of play is usually made by a leader who: has a lack of understanding of the security industry, is oblivious to the help they just received, or is totally trying to save face because they don't want anyone to know how lacking their program is. This leader doesn't understand that the deficiencies unearthed by the consulting company are great opportunities to grow the program and even use the data to gather more money for the budget.

Take this opportunity to get to the island faster. Not many companies out there have the budget to hire a consulting company. If your company gives you that opportunity, don't be too proud to take it. Learn from it, and become a more educated leader. Take it as an opportunity for your program, your team, and you to grow.

Empire ME Play

The empire ME play is usually a derivative of the buddy play, the GOAT play, and the gaslight play combined. If for some unknown reason you haven't gotten yourself or your team fired, or failed your company, what often happens is the people you hired don't have the knowledge to manage or lead a corporate security program. See, none of those folks have been to the island. You'll create excuses to hire more and more people to try to fill the holes, but the problem is that you're still playing games, and by now, your budget is running thin. You're unwilling to let your buddies go — you can't fire the people who do everything you demand without questioning (because it strokes your ego). So the next step is to keep building your empire.

Building an empire where the person in charge is pretty much stealing from the company is just a way to cover your tracks. It gives the sense that work is getting done, but it's not. It's all smoke and mirrors, a cover-up for your inability to get the corporate security program to the island. It's not efficient; it costs a tremendous amount of money and accomplishes very little.

Smart Play

If you are the leader, hire the best, most qualified person you can get for the money to help you start your program on the right foot. Do the great leader sales pitch, and always give the folks below you praise — and you'll know they all truly deserve it.

Hire the right captain to help you get to The Answer a lot faster!

Key Takeaways

Being the leader means being extra careful about how you appear to your peers from other departments and areas. It also means being a good role model for what is probably a team of contingent/contract security officers.

1 Avoid having a big ego and making enemies.

Keep in mind that your goal is to protect your company and their biggest assets: the people who work there and the company's products and services. **2**

3 Making an empire for yourself won't achieve your goal of building a great team and a great program.

Be smart about how you approach leadership. **4**

In the next chapter, you'll learn...

Corporate security fundamentals like how to get your program started and write a good mission statement.

Part IV: Corporate Security Fundamentals

The chapters ahead will give you an idea of what you must investigate and learn to prepare for upcoming opportunities. There's a good chance you've seen or heard of some of the concepts I'm about to introduce. If that's the case, awesome! This will just be a chance to review. If it's the first time you've heard of these concepts, this will be a quick breakdown of some of the things you should know before moving into the corporate business world.

Remember, in your role as either a member or leader of a corporate security team, or even a lone practitioner in a small company, *you* are a key steward of the company. The decisions you make and the procedures you put in place have a huge impact on the success of the company. You might be one of the few people in your company who understands threats and how to protect the most precious and valuable assets of any company... the people who work there!

Chapter 10: Basics of Corporate Physical Security

You'll notice there's a pattern to how I'm approaching this book. This is exactly how I would approach the process of making my company better or starting a new corporate security line of business within any company. My process is not the only one around, and there are plenty out there that would also make sense in any situation. This is just one way to set up a security program within a corporation.

Basic Getting Started List

I start a new corporate security program by looking at the items below, in this order:

- The mission of the company, leadership, and physical security
- Risk audit/questionnaire (What is our risk?)
- Minimum standards (What is the minimum requirement?)
  - Building (CPTED, lighting, locks, doors, physical)
  - Access control
  - CCTV

- □ Any other security systems in place
- □ Testing
- Policies (Why do we need to do this?)
- Procedures (How do we do this?)
- Guidelines (What guard rails can be dictated by the company while still leaving room for discretionary approaches?)
- Post orders (What does the officer do every day?)
- Protocols (How do we remedy an incident?)
- Briefings
  - □ Hand-Over/Take-Over Document
- Training
  - □ FTEs
  - □ CWs
  - □ Contract Guard Force (CGF)
    - □ CGF
    - □ Supervision
    - □ Management (SOM)
  - □ Visitors
  - □ Communications (up/down)
- Audit
  - □ Contracts (SOW)
  - □ CGF
  - □ Risks
  - □ Standards
    - □ Building
    - □ Access Control
    - □ CCTV
  - □ Policies
  - □ Procedures
  - □ Post Orders
  - □ Protocols
  - □ Training

At the same time, I would review:

- Guard Force Contract
- Real Estate Contract as it pertains to physical security

Visit the **"Downloads" on page 145** for a copy of this list!

Before you start with any of the ideas in the coming chapters, there are a couple of important things you must consider to prepare for the future of the security program.

Mission Statements

One of the first things you should do is think about the company's mission statement and the leadership's mission statement or what they want to get out of the program. Combine all of those and create a physical security mission statement. This will be useful as you go through all the concepts. Make sure all the upcoming concepts — the standards, policies, training, or anything you do going forward — agree with the mission statement.

Here's a couple examples of mission statements I've gotten to know well:

Facebook Global Security: "We keep the things that we value safe and secure while protecting the people, assets, and reputation of Facebook." The tag line is "Protecting the people, assets, and reputation."

Walt Disney World Security: "We enthusiastically promote a safe and secure environment that enables our Guests and Cast to experience the magic of Disney." The tag line is "Protecting the Magic."

Key Takeaways

Developing a good mission statement is at the core of how you build a good program.

1 A mission statement helps to solidify your values not just for your team, but also for the leadership and stakeholders you'll report to.

2 Mission statements don't have to be complicated.

3 Keep in mind that most people outside of security don't really understand what security does. A mission statement helps them understand your goals.

In the next chapter, you'll learn...

How to view risk through a corporate security lens.

Chapter 11: Risk Isn't Just a Board Game

As you step into your new position, either as a frontline operational manager or vice president of physical security, you'll need to know how to figure out your company's risk. This is important because you don't want to just spend the company's money without really understanding what your risk is. There are plenty of frameworks out there, and they're all very good. From the Threat and Hazard Identification and Risk Assessment (THIRA) process designed by the Department of Homeland Security to colorful risk assessment matrices to mathematical equations, risk audits, and questionnaires, they all work.

The key is that you know what they are, and when you're going through your interviews and, later, corporate career, you can talk about them. This doesn't mean that you need a doctorate in physical security. It simply means that you must have a basic understanding of what risk is for a corporation and be able to show the corporation that by hiring you, they're hiring the right person.

Reality Versus Consequences

An easy way to talk about risk is by focusing on the likelihood of an event happening versus the consequences. Ultimately, that will give you the answer to managing the situation by adding something to it, like a guard force, access control system, or other remedy. This may be a surprise, but avoiding or ignoring a risk altogether can be a legitimate option. If a risk to the company is so great that it will never be able to be mitigated, does a company really want to attempt to? On the other hand, maybe the risk is so low that ignoring it completely is an acceptable strategy. If it is insured, why should you be worried about the loss? Passing the burden to a separate entity like insurance or another third party might be the way to go. (I know, I know. This is a simple explanation, but remember, this book is about getting the job; it's not an entire class on risk.)

By the way, consultants are great to have if you're just starting to pinpoint all the resources you'll need. They'll give you the kitchen sink, usually a huge booklet with every security measure you can think of for your site. They do that because it protects them from liability, and when the shit hits the fan, they can say, "I told you so." Just remember: What they give you are just ideas that you could incorporate; always go back to your risk assessments and figure out what you truly *need*. Consultants will have you believe that you should mitigate every risk, and that's just not feasible, nor does it make you a good steward of your company.

Here's an example from my experience of a risk that is too high: running a data hall in a volatile country. You may let your corporation know that a certain risk is too high, but they could still choose to take it on. If that's the case, get the business owner's acceptance of the risk in writing. Having it in writing is key. It'll keep you out of some (but not all) problems that will surely arise in the future.

Another way to deal with risk is by ignoring it. Usually that comes with a place, building, or location that has no threats at all, and history has never shown any threats.

One of my favorite ways to deal with risk is to pass the burden to an insurance company. For example, if your warehouse is insured up to $1,000,000, and you only have $250,000 worth of inventory inside, you can easily let the insurance cover it instead of spending $1,000,000 a year on security. These are some ideas that you'll probably come across in the corporate world when it comes to risk, so you should be able to speak a little bit about it.

Throwing every possible solution at every physical security situation will cost your company a lot of money and cost you plenty of hair. Not every physical security situation requires thousands or millions of dollars. Take the time to understand the risk.

By the way, an easy way to show return on investment for your future corporation is to calculate avoided loss plus recoveries made divided by the cost of your proposed security program (technology, system, etc.). All corporations understand money, especially the C-suite folks, and that mathematical equation will help you sell them on what your security needs are for that risk.

$$\frac{\text{avoided loss} + \text{recoveries made}}{\text{cost of the security program}}$$

Reputational Risk

Another thing that's important to corporations today is reputational risk. This is a hard one to get around, but you must be aware of it for your interviews and, later, as you operate.

It's worth stating again: You will never be able to mitigate every risk that is out there, so don't try to do it. Do the best you can with what you have. You can measure reputational risk with a simple graph showing the length of time an event will be in the news cycle and the distance it will reach. Will it be in the news for one week or one year? Will it be shown locally or around the globe? Many maps and charts for determining reputational risk are available online.

I would personally rather focus on my answer to the media in the case of such an event than to try to fight every reputational risk that comes across my desk. It's an impossible task, for the most part, and one that I believe many security leaders out there are failing at by believing they can use money to stop reputational risk. This is probably time better spent meeting with your media relations, legal, and HR teams to talk about how you'd approach these incidents. This meeting should occur within three months of becoming the leader of your physical security program.

Key Takeaways

Avoiding loss without creating a cumbersome program that has something for even minor threats is the challenge of every corporate security professional.

1 You have to balance actual threat versus remote threat.

Consequences can sometimes be easier to deal with than building something to address a remote threat that has a small probability of happening. **2**

3 Your job might also entail managing reputational risk, and that requires a good system of partnerships and relationships.

In the next chapter, you'll learn...

Practical steps to create physical security standards.

Chapter 12: Show Me Your Standards

Another topic you should be versed in is physical security standards. What is the minimum you require to protect a location? I usually break down corporate physical security standards into six buckets:

1. Fence line
2. Lighting
3. Locks and doors
4. Intrusion Detection Systems (IDS)
5. Access control
6. Cameras

Building standards usually cover CPTED-based security (e.g., fences, lighting, locks, doors, and physical pieces). CPTED, in case you were wondering, is simply the use of the environment and architecture to help protect a location. You'll need to have a grasp of access control design, CCTV, and all the testing that goes with it. In your technical interviews, you'll have to be able to cover physical security standards. My definition of physical security standards is the minimum security measures that are put in place to deter, detect, defend, delay, or document unauthorized access to a building or area and protect my team members and company property and reputation. You can also find multiple CPTED sample surveys online to help you audit how you are doing and, ultimately, what you have learned before your interview. I'd also suggest you read more on CPTED.

Kicking off the standard process as fast as possible without the proper research will cause you major headaches a couple of years down the road. Companies like the ones I've mentioned move fast and grow fast. They don't just grow around your state now, or even in the United States. They're all over the world. This is the world we live in today. Standards are important because they give you an opportunity to keep everything the same. I'd even suggest you think about governance or someone who is an incredible project manager to help you through this process. You want to kick this off right. If you join a company that's behind the ball when it comes to standards or even governance, make suggestions! Just make sure the standard you set is broad enough that you can get parts, and service for those parts, throughout the world, but tight enough that someone working for you or the corporation can't just go out there and act like a freelancer, as my old friend Don Levonius used to say.

If you set the standards from the beginning, as soon as you have some influence, your life and everyone else's life around you will be so much better — not to mention it relieves you from answering an endless stream of questions due to confusion. The partners will always ask, "Where does that show in the standard?" If you put it together from the beginning, you'll be able to point it out.

Remember, put stuff you may need in the future in the standard document — just in case you have to point out where it lives.

Start with the Fence Line

Choosing the right fence will ultimately be left in your decision-making hands! You'll need to develop your standard, starting from the fence line inward.

- Will you have a fence line, bushes, or bollards, or will just the sidewalk do?
- If you do have a fence, what kind should it be?
- What kind of K rating should it have?
- Do you need a K rating on your fence line, or is the fence just to be used for demarcation?

You may be asked about this in your interview, so here's a quick fence breakdown:

- You should do your best to work with your business partners to come up with one fence line entrance only — maybe two if there's a delivery gate component to your operation. The goal here is to minimize the entrances to your location, which will make it a little more secured.
- There are plenty of fences out there. Of course, there is your everyday chain link fence. But as a security professional, you might want to think about an anti-climb/anti-cut fence that is at least eight feet tall (preferably, ten feet).
- Do you need a fence that is forge-welded and galvanized? Maybe, if you are off the main road, you need a fence that can withstand vehicle impact. You should take the time to investigate the ASTM F2656-15 standard. If you have a regular-sized vehicle traveling at 30 mph and the fence was able to stop it, it gets a 4K rating. At 40 mph, it gets an 8K rating, and at 50 mph, it gets a 12K rating.
- Think about the risk. What do you have inside that fence line? I've worked places where the risk was high, and we had a pretty robust fence system

with a 12K rating. I've also worked places where there was high pedestrian traffic and very few to no fences were necessary.

- Will you need to think about a gabion wall or even go as far as a ha-ha[1] for an uninterrupted view outside your fence line? By the way, ha-has and even gabion walls look ridiculous and are super expensive at any site in the world, with very few exceptions. I would advise against choosing either of these — unless you happen to be in a theater of war.
- Will you have a guard shack or not?
- Is your facility in a weather-challenged area, which means the guard shack needs to be sheltered?
- Does your guard shack need to be bullet resistant?
- What tools will you need inside the guard shack?
- Will you use an intercom system instead of an officer?
- Can the officer see from all sides?
- How about the entrance gate?
- Can the gates still operate if there's a power outage?
- Will you have some type of a hydraulic bollard, a K-rated gate arm, or even a hydraulic active barrier system?
- If you have pedestrian gates, you might want to look at having, at a minimum, a high-security padlock and an alarm contact with access control.

---

1 In case you didn't know, a ha-ha is a trench in front of or behind your fence line. It's what the military in World War I came up with to stop tanks. A gabion wall is a bunch of metal mesh boxes with rocks in them. Trust me, it sounds like something from medieval times, and I think it is.

Lighting

Lighting is extremely important as well. Not only does it keep the bad guys out, but it also helps your future company fight frivolous lawsuits when it comes to a safe environment. By the way, safety and security are not the same things. I'll talk more about the differences as we go.

Back to lighting! Strangely enough, in our world, lighting is measured by foot-candles (or lumens per square foot). One foot-candle equals one lumen per square foot, which equals approximately 10.75 lux. Lux is measured by how much light shines in a square meter. (I bet you didn't think you'd be doing some math today!) I learned this while working for a company that asked me to make sure we had at least one foot-candle per light at a parking lot. That was a fun day of looking at blueprints and light poles and figuring out how much each light pole shone. The great thing is that I was able to measure one of the pieces of CPTED to make sure all the lighting was working. (Make sure you tell your team to look for broken lights so they can get them fixed, or do a drive-by of your property at night to check the lights. You'll notice that plenty of them aren't working.)

- When we're talking about places like stairs, elevators, and ramps, there should be a minimum of 5 lumens of lighting, which equals approximately 54 lux.
- At a guard shack, you want 3 to 5 lumens so the officer can be seen, and they can look inside the vehicle and work safely around the guard shack.
- The wall and entranceways around garages, delivery docks, and buildings — or any access point for vehicles or pedestrians — should be 5 lumens, for the same reasons as the guard shack, plus it keeps the criminals away. Although I have used 1 to 2 lumens in huge parking lots before (like the ones at stadiums and parks), I'd say you should use 3 lumens for those.

- All building entrances should be at least
  10 foot-candles, and perimeter fence lines should
  be at least 2 lumens on both sides of the fence.
- Pedestrian lighting for walking paths should be
  somewhere between 12 and 15 feet high (so bad
  guys can't just break the light).

Locks and Doors

Locks and doors are another important part of the corporate physical security world. Every lock that must be defeated delays the bad guy from reaching their goal and allows the team to move to detect.

- The old school mortise lockset and a good
  commercial strike lock work well in most situations.

  "1865, Linus Yale, Jr. patented the cylinder
  mortise lock, which would revolutionize the
  industry. It used a pin tumbler cylinder with a
  series of spring-loaded pins that had to be raised
  to an exact height by the notches on a flat key
  before it would turn to operate the deadbolt. It
  was a system his father had worked on for years
  before, but it was Linus Yale, Jr.'s contribution
  to the manufacturing end that produced locks
  that were finely machined, mass produced, and
  difficult to override."[2]

---

2 Journal, Old House. "The Evolution of Entry Hardware." *Old House Journal Magazine*, 30 Dec. 2013, **www.oldhouseonline. com/gardens-and-exteriors/evolution-of-entry-hardware**.

- A maglock (electromagnetic) for sliding doors
  also works well, and I would suggest a fail-secure
  locking device so the door remains locked in case
  the power goes out.

> "An electromagnet is a magnet that is created
> when a current is moved through a wire with
> multiple coils around an iron core, or a solenoid
> (single coiled wire wrapped around a metal
> core). When the current is disrupted, the metal
> wire is no longer magnetized. Because of the
> very nature of an electromagnet, it cannot be
> fail-secure, which means that in the result of
> an emergency or power outage, the doors will
> unlock. The built-in feature of unlocking in the
> result of a power outage (referred to as fail-safe)
> was the founding idea of the electromagnet. The
> lock was first made as a commissioned safety
> feature for the Montreal Forum in Quebec,
> Canada. The issue they were made to solve was
> the threat of doors being locked in the event of
> an emergency. The fear was that in the event of
> a fire, staff would have to go to all the doors and
> unlock them, or simply leave every door in the
> building unlocked."[3]

- I would also add a latch guard door plate right
  at the lock-level at every out-swinging door,
  especially if they are leading to the outside of the
  building. Obviously, the latch guard is so people
  don't try the old credit card trick on your doors.
- Doors should be commercial and solid. It makes
  no sense to have a door that does not withstand

---

3 Ralph. "Everything You Need To Know About Magnetic Locks."
United Locksmith, 8 Dec. 2017, **unitedlocksmith.net/blog/
everything-you-need-to-know-about-magnetic-locks**.

the abuse of everyday use and will not help protect anything.

- When it comes to mantraps or anti-passback devices, obviously a two-door system that won't allow you to open a door while the first door is open is nice; however, technology has moved forward and a turnstile kind of entryway is best.
- I love the "beam me up, Scotty" style doors that the Boon Edam Tourlock or Circlelock doors offer. Only one person in at a time!
- Automatic door closers with card readers, an electric locking system, and door contacts are always a go.
- When it comes to emergency doors, try looking into delayed egress. Delayed egress doors alarm and delay before automatically opening in an emergency. They just buy security a couple more seconds.
- As an addition, I suggest you place a sounder with a strobe at every high-risk door.

Intrusion Detection Systems (IDS)

- When it comes to IDS, you may want to study up on systems like IR beams and shower along with camera systems that produce a pixel change and use analytics. (There are others like Southwest Microwave, Spotter RF, Jemez, Argus (RF), fiber and underground systems that you might want to look at as well.)
- If you place a system like a Southwest Microwave on a fence that is next to too much wildlife, trees or some type of low bushes, it won't work as well due to all the noise (alarms) the system will encounter.
- What you'll find is that not all systems work for all purposes. Some work better in a clear, open

area (like a Spotter RF), some work better in cities (like beams and showers), some work better right on the fence, and others just don't work at all for what you're trying to do. That's why it's important to study up on possible systems, learn their uses, and understand the environment where each would work best.

- Think about the application, ask a lot of questions, do your research, and go for the right tool for the job.

Access Control

It's imperative in today's world that you use an access control system. It will help you better protect your property, minimize risk, and provide you with data. Many times, due to compliance bodies like ISO and SOC, you'll need the system to be certified. I'd almost say that this is a must, and it must be at the top of your list of security systems to implement. Plus, an access control system gets rid of pesky keys. Imagine that a master key is lost for your building and you have to re-key every door. That would be costly... and a great way to sell your leaders on the need for an access control system.

- When implemented, I'd also set it up to be role-based — unless you are a military facility, then I would go with the mandatory rule where only the owner or their appointee can manage access. (FYI: "Role-based" means based on your job title. The higher the job title, the more access you have.)
- As you study up on access control, learn about the importance of having an open standard system so you can plug other systems, like cameras, into it.
- Take the time to learn how to add doors, groups, and individuals and, ultimately, how to connect them all.

- Understand the differences between role-based and space-based clearances.
- What is the significance of Door Held Open (DHO), Door Forced Open (DFO), Door Open (DO), masking, shunting, etc.? How do they affect the business and, more importantly in this case, the security posture?
- Look into websites for access control companies like Lenel and CCure, and while you're at it, research the different readers that are available, like card (works with multiple technologies), biometric, facial, and retina.
- You'll never be able to get away from good ol' keys. How you manage them is also important. There are systems out there that use access control to remove and use keys. I've been using Traka since at least 2011, and it works great. Keeps people accountable for doing the right thing and taking care of them, and it also reminds them that the keys are traceable. The system will even alarm and send out emails when the keys aren't returned at the time that was specified within the system.

Cameras

How about cameras? Here's a little bit of background:

> "The first digital security camera systems were used by the military for security and reconnaissance. In 1980, the same camera technology that brought soap operas to televisions nationwide also helped protect businesses against fraud and theft."[4]

---

4 "The History of Video Cameras." *CCTV Camera World*, www.cctvcameraworld.com/the-history-of-video-cameras.html.

The great thing about cameras today is that they have definitely surpassed the old analog days — though many folks would say there's still a need for analog, and, in some cases, I concur.

- As you explore cameras, camera software, camera analytical systems, etc., study up on frames per second and determine the minimum you'd like to have. I like a minimum of 30, though many companies run at 15, and many more run at even fewer, in which case it starts to become pointless. I prefer 30 as it allows the frame to be slow enough that I can see better recognition. By the way, the reason most companies use fewer frames per second is because of storage capability.
- Another important specification of the camera is the number of pixels it has. I wouldn't go any less than 10 megapixels, though a lot of companies use two to eight without a problem. Once again, it's all about storage capacity and, in this case, distance.
- You should also learn about the new cameras and their analytical capabilities, especially in the use of intrusion detection.
- Not all cameras are the same, and not all of them work well at night or when they are facing some kind of light, like the sun or a streetlight. Read a little about that as well.
- Some cameras are stored in DVR, some NVR, and a lot these days are moving to the cloud for more space. Take the time to look at the differences. There's plenty of software out there, and ultimately, they're almost the same. It's all about preference and, in some cases, price.
- I've used Open Eye, Genetec, exacqVision, and Avigilon to name a few. Check them out for some education.

Key Takeaways

Security standards get real when you're dealing with building a program. You have to master a great deal of practical knowledge in order to build a system with the right components.

1	Begin with the fence line since perimeter security is a core standard. Then work from the fence line in and think about lighting.
2	Doors and locks have different standards based on what type of structure you're responsible for.
3	Intrusion Detection Systems (IDS) can be a core component of some types of properties, but it depends on what you're protecting.
4	Camera technology changes frequently, but core basics will remain stable over time.

In the next chapter, you'll learn...

The importance of documentation. You'll need to be able to understand and manage everything from post orders to training documentation.

Chapter 13: Your Guard Force

As you move from the government side of the world to corporate, there's a good chance you'll be managing a contract, unless you go to a company that has their own proprietary security. In proprietary security, you directly manage the HR and other challenges with your guard force. There are discussions now and then about whether a company should go with their own proprietary security or a contract guard force. These are the top two things that usually block a company from creating their own proprietary security force:

1. The cost of insurance and benefits
2. Dealing with HR issues like hiring and firing

Contract Guard Force Statement of Work

Because security is not a true career path in the United States, though it is in many European countries, in some areas, it's very difficult to get qualified, willing, energetic, excited, educated, and properly trained folks that want to do the security job for the pay. So, in probably 80% of the cases (my personal guess), a company decides to go with an outside vendor to deal with all the issues that come with a security guard force.

When you are dealing with a contract guard force company, it is important to understand that you do not manage their people. You usually work with a Security Operations Manager from that company as your partner, and they manage their people. You only have the power to manage the contract. It's important to understand this because if you don't, you'll be in the middle of a co-employment issue, which is illegal.

As a Security Manager for your company, you will have the rights and the obligations as the employer to lead the security team. The Security Operations Manager for that contract guard force company is the only one that can manage the personnel-related functions, such as HR and payroll issues, for the guard force. So, how do I manage the contract guard force, you may ask?

KPIs and SLAs

While managing the contract, agreement, or, as it's called in many cases, the Statement of Work (SOW), make sure to add Key Performance Indicators (KPIs) and Service Level Agreements (SLAs). KPIs and SLAs are what will allow you to measure how well the contract guard force you hired is doing.

Examples of KPIs include:

- Dropped shifts
- Open positions
- Officer attrition
- Recruiting yield
- Workforce utilization
- Training completed and documented
- Invoice and billing accuracy
- Management visits
- Intrusion test results
- Rotation work schedules
- Monthly reports
- Quarterly reports

- Quarterly business review (QBR) minutes
- And any others your leaders, the company, or you may desire (and the contract guard force company agrees to)

Here are some examples of SLAs:

- Failure to adhere to personnel placement requirements
- Failure to ensure all personnel are in possession of required documentation and equipment
- Incident notification
- Incident updates
- Unauthorized access
- Failure to adhere to the contract guard force's Code of Conduct
- The contract guard force's failure to provide Service Credit on Applicable Invoice
- Self-audit tables
- Monthly report
- Shift coverage
- Guard sleeping on duty
- Patrols conducted
- Contract guard force-triggered alarms
- Alarm acknowledgment
- Alarm SLA breach
- Annual recertification training
- Monthly/quarterly attrition
- Training
- And any others your leaders, the company, or you may desire (and the contract guard force company agrees to)

In this kind of work, and within the agreement, you may only speak to the Security Operations Manager for the contract guard force company, and not directly to the officers, to give any orders or training. Be cautious of that and always keep it in the back of your mind. The contract guard force does not work for you. The Security Operations Manager for that contract guard force is essentially your partner in your security effort, and you may only speak to them to give directions, and then, in return, they will speak to their security officers about what you requested.

There are some challenges to the contract guard force business. The folks that come into leadership positions often aren't prepared to take on the task. They're all amazing folks who, like you, come from the military, law enforcement, or federal jobs and are just thrown into the fire of the contract guard force business without the proper training or tools. Anyone who spent 20, 25, 30-plus years in any of these fields before starting a second career is incredible. I can just imagine what it's like to work for the government for that long — any type of government.

They can all do the job, but without the proper training and tools, you'll find yourself training those officers because their company failed to put money and time into training before bringing them out to your property.

Another challenge you will find with third-party vendors or contract guard forces is that they have difficulty keeping track of operating hours, which delays their billing, and many times, the numbers are inflated. They'll have a difficult time finding the right people for the job and filling positions for a lot of the hours requested while they're working for you. You'll have to keep an eye on this because you'll likely still be billed for it.

Contract guard forces have a really difficult time finding amazing people because the security field, as I mentioned before, is not really a career in the United States. It's usually a job that you joined because a friend joined, or maybe because it paid $0.50 more than any other job in your community. Many of the folks who work in the contract guard force as an officer usually only have a high school diploma or GED. Many of them come from lower-income homes, and many have challenges of their own to fight through. You'll have to constantly manage that contract to make sure that the KPIs and SLAs are met.

Sadly, the contract guard force business has become a sales job, and their job is to sell you bodies to fulfill positions. Most companies that go into the contract guard force business don't take the time to train their people properly, continue to find ways to create bonuses for their higher tiers of leadership, and usually do it over the cost of your business.

You'll have to keep an eye on overtime percentages (which should be around 2% or less), the number of flex staff members being used, and opened and unstaffed posts (also known as dark posts), and you'll have to make sure through the SLAs that you're keeping up with the contract guard force vendor credits they should be giving back to you.

The items above are just a few you should be looking for in your Quarterly Business Review (QBR). Please educate yourself concerning contracts and agreements with a third-party contract guard force. Take the time to learn what the market is requesting in billable hours. Contract guard force companies will upsell you and take all the money they possibly can. Come to the negotiation table prepared and understand what the local market is charging. Basically, for about 90% of your agreement with them, you're truly just paying for bodies to cover your company from some liabilities. This is the exact reason why some companies do choose to have their own proprietary security. Proprietary security is usually better trained, more prepared, better with customer service, and perform better when dealing with major emergency incidents. Take the time to think about the direction you would like to go and how you would sell it to the C-suite.

I've had the opportunity to work on both sides, and both have their merits. I promise you will be extremely valuable for understanding their business and, at the same time, being able to manage the contract.

Key Takeaways

The people aspect of your guard force will vary depending on whether or not you're using a proprietary force.

1 If your company has proprietary security, you'll directly manage the HR and other challenges with your guard force.

2 A contract guard force will have its own challenges, specifically that you really only control the relationship with the Security Operations Manager and how you measure outcomes.

In the next chapter, you'll learn...

About working with HR and higher leadership to develop policies and procedures specific to your company.

Chapter 14: Documentation and Guidance

You'd think that corporations would have a tremendous number of policies, procedures, and guidelines to help them navigate through the land mines of the corporate world.

More often than not, you'd be wrong.

Some do have a heavy approach to those, but for the most part, companies today are pretty light on them, especially the ones that deal with security. In today's corporate world, security is kind of a bad word. In my experience, most corporations run very open campuses that allow for free flow of movement and very minimal security impact to operations. With that in mind, companies tend to keep in place basic policies, procedures, and guidelines that keep them out of the courtroom.

The most common security questions today are about metal detecting, undercover security folks with guns, and a heavy security approach (like performing bag checks). The interesting thing is that most companies don't want to be part of any of those things. It'll be up to you to work with higher leadership to design policies, procedures, and discretionary guidelines that will allow you to operate safely but openly. There's always heavy communication with HR and the company lawyers on almost every employee-related incident. There's also a heavy relationship with HR and the lawyers when it comes to security approaches. The key point here is that in no way, shape, or form can you take policies that were written behind federal, state, and local statutes and use them in the corporate world. The ideas from your current career can definitely be used as a starting point in a conversation, but make sure you always involve HR and your company's lawyers so you don't get into trouble. An example would be trying to write a policy on the use of force in the corporate world — a corporation should never write a policy on the use of force.

I usually say that no policy needs to be written when it's already a federal mandate or constitutional right.

Security Post Orders

When it comes to posting orders for security officers, they're usually put together by the contract guard force that you hire. Then you add your proprietary pieces to it, such as a policy or the procedures of a security system you are using, and give it back to the guard force contract company to finalize. Some corporations will write all the post orders for a contract guard force. Be careful with that because it leaves you open for liability.

Protocols

Like post orders, protocols are designed the same way. The contract guard force company starts with it, you fill in some of your company stuff, then you give it back to the contract guard force company to finalize and educate their team. Of course, with all the things I previously mentioned in mind, you must audit. I'd suggest you audit those processes every six months so you can make sure they're up to date and check for any revisions needed. You should always audit your program — especially the training.

Training

Training for a contract guard force should always be provided by the contract guard force company when an officer starts. The beginning training should be 40 hours at the contract guard force company's expense. The additional hours can be billed to you. You should always emphasize to the contract guard force companies that they should be doing their training on shift with minimal allowable overtime. Unlike the military, group training should be done no more than 16 hours a year. Most major companies I have worked for only did eight hours of group training a year, and the rest were all during briefings or hip-pocket training while on shift and on post.

I highly suggest that you train on security customer service basics because it's truly one of the most important things I've learned in my corporate security career. There's no room for a bouncer mentality in the corporate world. To create an awesome security team, I like to focus on the following ten items.

10 Recommendations for an Awesome Security Team

1	Make eye contact and smile at everyone! Everyone loves a smiling person.
2	Greet and welcome everyone. Be the ambassador!
3	Seek out team member (people) contact. Introduce yourself and create new friendships!
4	Provide immediate service recovery. It's okay to not be perfect, but quickly fix it with no excuses!
5	Always display appropriate body language. Be the professional you know you can be!
6	Create an awesome workplace experience for all. It starts with you!
7	Express thanks whenever possible. Thank people for almost anything and tell them how wonderful a job they're doing!
8	Observation skills. Love to observe people. People-watching is fun!
9	Radio communications. Simple and to the point. Tell me what you see! What's the situation?
10	Lastly, report writing. The truth lies here!

I promise you the soft approach will always work for every type of security team.

I'll end this chapter with a post I put up on LinkedIn that was so dear to me, and I hope this resonates with you when it comes to your team:

Don't ever be afraid to educate your team...

- I want my team members to get the best and as much education as my budget can afford and the company allows.
- If they fly away, they will be better representatives of my leadership and my company, and they will be the most prepared in a room.
- If they surpass me in my career, I will be a proud peer and colleague, and I will continue to support them every year.
- I'll never know when the one that used to work for me becomes the best leader I'll ever have.

Again, I would be proud, because I know the training opportunities I afforded them made them a better leader than I am today and a future leader of the most prepared in a room.

Key Takeaways

Most companies prefer a soft approach to security now, so you'll work with HR and higher leadership to design policies, procedures, and guidelines that will allow you to operate safely but openly.

1 If you hire a contract guard force, they generally provide post orders and protocols, but you'll add the proprietary pieces.

2 Always audit your program, especially the training; aim to check every 6 months for any changes that may be needed.

3 Train your security team in basic customer service and encourage a soft approach.

In the next chapter, you'll learn...

Data management will be a key part of your new role.

Chapter 15: It's All About Data!

Understanding data and how it works in your favor is extremely important for a security leader in the corporate world. There's a good chance that anyone you have to talk to in order to garner money for your security program will be data-driven and will need to see the data before you get any funding.

Security Events

As you step into your new company, start keeping tabs of everything that goes on so you can start forming data sets. When it comes to your security operation, you'll want to know how many security events the company has had. Use a program that will easily get you the who, what, why, when, and how of every security event. You'll need that in case you have to raise money for more officers or security systems.

> The concept is simple:
> more events = more officers.

These events can be anything that is important to your company, your leader, or yourself. The different events can be as simple as:

- Team member assist
- Careless situation/behavior
- Injury
- Stolen item/theft
- Missing item
- Threat
- Inappropriate comments
- Suspicious incident
- Complaint
- Building/door check
- Unsecured
- Disturbance
- Fire
- Alarm
- Agency assist
- Assist with termination
- Property report
- Copyright infringement
- Violation of company policy
- Illness
- Animal incident
- Trespass
- AED deployment
- 9-1-1 response
- Any other event you'd like to add to start gathering the data you need to set your budget up for success.

Data Points You'll Want to Know

Security Systems

These are some of the things you should be thinking about when it comes to security systems (though there's plenty more data you can collect):

- The system's up and downtime — everything from your CCTV to where you hold the data, either through DVR, NVR, or the cloud
- The up and downtime for your intrusion detection systems, access control systems, security panels, network outages, and cameras

Building Entry and Exit

- How many are coming in and out?
- How many badges do you have printed?
- How many employees are losing their badges?
- Where are they going within the building?

Alarms

- Door Held Open (DHO) is an alarm that is set through your access control system that alarms security when an access-controlled door has been left open for longer than a set period of time. I'd suggest no more than 10 seconds at a high-security area, 30 seconds at a medium-security area, and 60 seconds at a low-security area.
- Door Forced Open (DFO) is an alarm that is set through your access control system that alarms security to an access-controlled door that was opened without using a badge or the proper opening method.

- Anti-passback alarms, masking, and everything else that I mentioned previously. Anti-passback (APB) is an alarm that is set to alert when multiple people have entered a location with only one key entry. For an APB, you'll need extra hardware and software to implement in your access control system.

You can use a lot of those alarms to educate your team members on what to do and what not to do at your locations. I might even suggest that you start a security program that would educate the employees of your company on a minimum monthly basis. This program can be a mirror copy of the "If You See Something, Say Something" program from the Department of Homeland Security. You can use this data to educate them on the right things to do when it comes to following access control policies, what is suspicious, how to help us protect our property, and so on. Your imagination is your only blocker.

By the way, the program will be a great way to show security's value to leadership and all team members.

Key Takeaways

Data you collect via the systems you control can be a good way to get a real idea of how your program is functioning. This data can also be a way to tell the story of your program to stakeholders and your leadership.

1 Design data around the story you want to tell.

2 Capture data for a set period of time before analyzing it. Usually 90 days, but if the data has been collected prior to your arrival, you can do year-over-year and month-over-month assessments.

3 Data can sometimes reveal shortcomings with your own program, and you should be prepared to address them.

In the next chapter, you'll learn...

We'll wrap things up and give you some further resources and tips for the exciting journey you're about to begin — your career in corporate security!

Wrap Up and Resources

Maybe Corporate Security Isn't for You

The truth of the matter is that corporate security isn't for everyone. There's a temperament, a style, and a cultural and career background that may not fit the corporate world. Even today, I sometimes dream about my past as a police officer. I need the mission. There are plenty of times in the corporate security world that the mission is lost, or it's not very clear, or it just doesn't carry the same weight as my mission once did.

I sometimes have a tremendous yearning to be part of a squad again. The competition among us helped unify and drive us to be better. I reminisce about times when I was kicking down the bad guy's door to save a screaming woman. I want the investigation or a traffic stop that leads to a significant arrest. I miss chasing the criminal on the run, knocking on doors to find a warrant runner, and even just hanging at my 3:00 a.m. coffee spot where the squad and I used to meet to chat about our day with our favorite barista. I miss hanging out with my squad on our days off and living that lifestyle — the sheepdog lifestyle. Sadly, I even miss going to court, and, as anyone who has been a police officer will tell you, going to court is probably one of the worst parts of being a cop.

I wasn't afraid of anything or anybody because I knew I always had someone just like me who was willing to throw their life on the line as I would for them. My squad had my back, and I had theirs. We took care of our problems internally and with each other.

Here's the thing: If you still feel like you have many years left of what I just mentioned, then corporate security may not be for you. Now, with what I'm about to say, I don't mean to paint corporate security with a broad brush; these are my experiences and opinion alone.

In the corporate security world, you'll never kick down the bad guys' door. You'll never chase the criminal or make an arrest again. You'll never pursue a warrant runner, and you'll surely never again be able to speak freely about your job at your favorite coffee spot. The times of hanging out with your squad or war buddies or firehouse or ambulance team are over. There won't be much hanging out with the work team. You'll start to become afraid and less brave than you used to be. You'll question or, at least, be way more careful with your interactions at work. There will be times when you won't be able to take care of work issues with the person directly, and HR will be brought in. You may never again experience the feeling of adrenaline pumping through your veins or the camaraderie of a team that relies on one another for everything.

There's competition in the corporate security world as well, but it's about who did more. Not everyone is looking for ways to praise or lift up their team, so it tends to be about tooting your own horn. Unfortunately, bonuses are attached to the individual work and not the teamwork. Because of that, there are plenty of people who are willing to do you wrong for the bonus or to move up in the company. I know there are plenty of people in the military, law enforcement, emergency services, and federal jobs who are willing to do the same, but luckily, I've never had that experience.

That is why, especially if you are coming out of the military, law enforcement may be the right choice for you — not corporate security. If you've never felt that adrenaline or camaraderie, or you are over it, then corporate security may be for you. Truth be told, I was not a police officer long enough to have such deep feelings for the career that they hindered me in the corporate security world. It was easy for me to navigate in and out of it. But there are plenty of folks who come into corporate security from the military, law enforcement, fire and rescue, federal careers, and so on, who cannot make the mental switch to be successful. I wrote this book to help, and I'd be remiss if I didn't acknowledge this: Corporate security is *not* for everyone.

Carlos' Top 25 Tips

1. Really assess and ask yourself if corporate security is right for you. Will you miss the action of law enforcement or the military?
2. Prepare your family for a new life and a new you.
3. Figure out why you want to transition into corporate security. It'll save you headaches in the future.
4. Start your transition process today. If you start tomorrow, you'll be a day behind another person who is as well, if not more, qualified than you.
5. Get any certifications you think will help boost your skills or confidence (especially from ASIS).
6. Clean up your social media.
7. You can't be shy in the career transition game. You must reach out to people and make friends.
8. Every person you meet from now on could be hiring you in the future. Remember that!
9. The odds of getting the job if the hiring manager doesn't know you or know about you are slim to none.
10. You can't use the same resume for every job you apply for. An ordinary resume gets you an ordinary job. Look at the job description and tailor your resume for it.
11. Translate any jargon in your resume or cover letter into something folks in the corporate world can understand, and remember it for the interview.
12. Focus on the line of business within corporate security that your career best mirrors.
13. Focus on a company that best aligns with your values and personal culture.
14. If you focus on money as you're transitioning, the job you want will not come.
15. Preparing for an interview is key. Don't prepare for the interview if you don't want the job.

16. Your interviewer is your audience. Tell them what you think they want to hear — not what makes you feel good about yourself.
17. Use the STAR method for interviewing, and be the star of the interview process.
18. No interview is ever wasted, even if you don't get the job.
19. Be yourself, and never compare yourself to others or where they have gone since their transition.
20. Never miss the opportunity to introduce yourself and build a new relationship.
21. Master the basics of corporate security.
22. Know *current* best practices for systems and technology.
23. Update your wardrobe.
24. Understand how corporations view risk and consequence.
25. Follow *The Corporate Security Translator* and listen to our podcasts! You'll learn lots from actual people who successfully transitioned into corporate security.

Additional Advice

Scott Vedder

"I am a proud civilian advocate for veterans and anyone transitioning into a new job in the corporate workforce. In my experience conducting 5,000+ interviews, including as a corporate security recruiter for a Fortune 100 company, I recognized that people needed help and direction to be successful and feel confident in the job application process. This was especially true for veterans who were typically not familiar with applying for jobs at all! My father and grandfather both served in the United States Army and no one helped them in their transition. I wrote *Signs of a Great Résumé* and *Signs of a Great Interview* to provide answers to the most common questions veterans ask and to share my best tips from the recruiter's side of the interview desk."

- *Signs of a Great Résumé: Veterans Edition: How to Write a Résumé that Speaks for Itself* **www.amazon.com/gp/aw/d/149491834X/**
- *Signs of a Great Interview: Veterans Edition: How to Tell a Story that Speaks for Itself* **www.amazon.com/dp/B08VYLP3JJ/**

Scott R Wolford CPP, CPC

Beyond the Blue Coaching

"When I retired from public service, I foundered for many months before finding my way into a rewarding private sector career. If only I'd had a resource like *So, You Want to Get into Corporate Security?* when I was making my transition, I would have been able to set my course with confidence. Carlos uses his own experience transitioning from the military to law enforcement and the private sector, as well as the experiences of experts from many backgrounds, to guide the transitioning professional in their journey. Don't reinvent the wheel! Learn from those who have successfully made the switch. Highly recommended!"

Scot Walker

"After almost 20 years in the military and federal law enforcement, I decided I better prepare for my next career, which would be in the private sector. Through networking with the university I attended and LinkedIn, I developed critical relationships with business leaders who would be instrumental in my development as a person, leader, and critical thinker, ultimately giving me the opportunity to explore new opportunities. Now I help others with their transition, giving back to the institution that contributed to my success. I am eternally grateful to everyone who took the time to teach me along the way."

John Lineweaver

"My transition from the military to the corporate security world was a natural progression for me. Having served as a Marine Embassy Guard and Military Police Auxiliary, I had the essentials to begin my work in commercial Class A security. I found security work interesting, rewarding, and ever changing. One of the best things about the field was the constant contact with the public; I've always enjoyed helping others and still do to this day. As my career progressed from commercial, hospitality, critical infrastructure protection, and finally the tech industry, I found that earning promotions and assignments was a direct result of developing a deeper understanding of the need to balance security with the operational business needs.

"A key takeaway: Learn the business side and how to develop your security program into a value add for your organization. Think outside of the box and not just 'barricades and barbed wire.' Take the time to build relationships along the way, and above all else, have fun!"

Rhett Weddell

"Great book designed to *help* transitioning professionals. Number one: family! My family — Katrina, Ashley, Megan and Alex(andra) — served the US Army Military Police Corps for 23+ years, and YES, families serve as much or more than the service members. What? How can that be? Service members train; we understand and execute the mission without a second thought while families serve in a supporting role. My career included 18 or so relocations, multiple schools (some in the same year), careers on hold, and years without friends, family, or a mall! All for the shared goal of selfless service. I salute my family and other military families for their commitment and would ask anyone transitioning to talk through your next dream, goal, or aspiration with your family. Number two: Not all money is good money! Do what you love.

"Of the troops and for the troops!"

Richard P. Mullan

"I've had the honor of mentoring many new professionals and transitioning military and law enforcement members as they explore career pathing in the corporate security profession. The discussions begin with the concept or understanding that a career path is not a straight line, much like a ladder with one way up. My life's experience has taught me that career paths are more of a lattice woven in with all the turns and intersections faced during the course of a career. Your professional development, education, work experience, areas of expertise, transferable skills, and professional network enable you to navigate career opportunities as they avail themselves on your journey. The Corporate Security Translator, Carlos Francisco, provides invaluable career coaching and insight to successfully navigate your career transition."

Al Bora

"At age 18, I stood on the famous 'yellow footprints' at Marine Corps Recruit Training taking my first steps on my journey to become a United States Marine. Almost 20 years later, I found myself standing on another set of 'yellow footprints,' this time to take my first steps into corporate security. While my transition into the corporate world was challenging, the values I learned in the military helped me stay focused, execute, and ultimately achieve success. The best advice I ever received during this process was to 'burn the ships' and not look back with any regret! In other words, fully commit to your transition goals. Transitioning, while challenging, is also extremely liberating. Embrace the challenge, commit to your goals, and enjoy the journey!"

Downloads

Chapter 5: The Interview

- Interview Sheets (Interview Cheat Sheet, Interview Talking Points)

Chapter 10: Basics of Corporate Physical Security

- Basic Getting Started List

Chapter 12: Show Me Your Standards

- Fence Line Checklist

Downloads are available on the How2Conquer website:

rebrand.ly/CorpSecDownloads

Resources to Check Out

Podcasts and YouTube

Francisco, Carlos. "The Corporate Security Translator."
    YouTube, **www.youtube.com/channel/UCIFqUsKf1xT-T7sN8COfEXg**.
Francisco, Carlos. "The Corporate Security Translator
    Podcast." Buzzsprout, **www.buzzsprout.com/1560995**.

Books

Vedder, Scott. *Signs of a Great Résumé: Veterans Edition:
    How to Write a Résumé That Speaks for Itself.*
    CreateSpace Independent Publishing Platform, 2014.

Websites

"How Veterans Can Write a Great LinkedIn Profile."
    WeHireHeroes, 23 Dec. 2018, **wehireheroes.com/
    blog/how-veterans-can-write-a-great-linkedin-profile**.

Acknowledgments

A special thanks to the wonderful leaders and teammates I've had throughout my career who took the time to throw a word or two into this book and share a piece of their adventure as they moved from government to corporate security:

Joshua Bartke
Altaf Bora
Greg Bowman
John Lineweaver
Doug Mikatarian
Richard Mullan
Rickey Ricks
Scott Vedder
Scot Walker
Rhett Weddell
Scott Wolford

About the Author

Carlos Francisco has spent over two decades leading security teams at some of the largest corporations in the world, including Walt Disney World Resort, Amazon, and Facebook, as well as at major international events such as Super Bowl 50, Major League Baseball, National Basketball Association, World-Class Marathons, and many more.

Carlos holds a bachelor's degree in Criminal Justice and a Security Management certificate from the University of Central Florida, as well as a masters' degree in Emergency and Disaster Management from American Military University. He is a Certified Protection Professional (CPP) and holds a certificate for Infrastructure Protection from Texas A&M Engineering Extension Service.

When he's not working, Carlos volunteers his time as a Big Brother with Big Brothers Big Sisters and contributes to his community at Second Harvest, Junior Achievement, and Habitat for Humanity. He loves to spend time with his family, especially his son Jax.

Reading Group Discussion Questions

1. Why do you want to transition to corporate security? What does security mean to you?
2. If you took a personality test, what do you think it would reveal to a potential employer?
3. Why should you try to be "everyone's best friend"? Who in your reading group might be helpful or just nice to keep in touch with?
4. Do you find that you use a lot of jargon in your everyday speech? What are the benefits and the downfalls of using jargon?
5. What were you most surprised to learn about the corporate world?
6. What is culture-shifting? Have you ever "embraced the chameleon"?
7. What do you think you'd do well in corporate security? What do you think you'll need to work on most as you prepare to transition into your new career?
8. Why might you need to enlist professional help with your resume?
9. What is the STAR method? Share an example you could use in an interview!
10. What are the benefits of using a contract guard force?
11. How would you explain CPTED to someone outside corporate security?
12. What are some ways to monitor and track the performance of a contract guard force?
13. Has reading *So, You Want to Get into Corporate Security?* affected the way you think about or approach your current role?

www.ingramcontent.com/pod-product-compliance
Lightning Source LLC
Chambersburg PA
CBHW071419210326
41597CB00020B/3573